NORSE AMERICA

OXFORD UNIVERSITY PRESS PUBLICATIONS BY GORDON CAMPBELL

As author

The Oxford Dictionary of the Renaissance
Renaissance Art and Architecture
John Milton: Life, Work and Thought (co-author)
Milton and the Manuscript of 'De Doctrina Christiana' (co-author)
Very Interesting People: John Milton
Bible: The Story of the King James Version
The Hermit in the Garden: From Imperial Rome to Ornamental Gnome
A Short History of Gardens

As editor

The Oxford Illustrated History of the Renaissance
The Holy Bible: Quatercentenary Edition
The Grove Encyclopedia of Decorative Arts (2 vols)
The Grove Encyclopedia of Classical Art and Architecture (2 vols)
The Grove Encyclopedia of Northern Renaissance Art (3 vols)
Renaissance Studies (10 vols)
The Review of English Studies (13 vols)
The Complete Works of John Milton (13 vols, in progress)
W. R. Parker, *Milton: a Biography* (2 vols)
Ben Jonson, *The Alchemist and Other Plays*

As contributor

Grove Art Online
The Oxford Chronology of English Literature
The Oxford Companion to English Literature
The Oxford Companion to the Garden
The Oxford Dictionary of National Biography
The Oxford Dictionary of the Christian Church
The Oxford English Dictionary

GORDON CAMPBELL

NORSE
AMERICA

the story of a founding myth

OXFORD
UNIVERSITY PRESS

OXFORD

UNIVERSITY PRESS

Great Clarendon Street, Oxford, OX2 6DP,
United Kingdom

Oxford University Press is a department of the University of Oxford.
It furthers the University's objective of excellence in research, scholarship,
and education by publishing worldwide. Oxford is a registered trade mark of
Oxford University Press in the UK and in certain other countries

Published in the United States of America by Oxford University Press
198 Madison Avenue, New York, NY 10016, United States of America

British Library Cataloguing in Publication Data
Data available

Library of Congress Control Number: 2020950723

ISBN 978–0–19–886155–3

Printed and bound in Great Britain by
Clays Ltd, Elcograf S.p.A.

For the Skrælings

PREFACE AND
ACKNOWLEDGEMENTS

My first academic post was at Aarhus University in Denmark, where I studied Danish and began to explore the Nordic world. In the intervening decades I have been able to travel in the Nordic homelands, settlement areas, and trading centres: in the east, Novgorod and Kiev, the Byzantine Empire and the Islamic Caliphate; in the south, the British and Irish settlements, Normandy, and Brittany; in the north, Svalbard (where no indisputable evidence of a Norse presence has been found); and in the west, the Faeroes, Iceland, Greenland, and Canada—and always visiting museums as I travelled. Sometimes evidence of a Norse presence is thin: in St Kilda, for example, Old Norse place names have not so far been supported by archaeology, and in Maine, the historic significance of a solitary Norse coin is debated. The Maine State Museum that holds this coin is also the home of the Spirit Pond Runestones, which have roused strong emotions. In the case of other American runestones, such the Heavener Runestone in Oklahoma and the Kensington Runestone in Minnesota, I have had to be diplomatic in the face of entrenched local beliefs about the circumstances of their composition. The most important remote site supported by solid archaeological evidence is L'Anse aux Meadows, on the northern tip of Newfoundland, and the discovery of that site in the 1960s planted the seed that eventually grew into a central narrative of this book. Research continues apace. Sites on Baffin Island and in Labrador are full of promise, but they have not yet been fully investigated. Other sites (Ungava Bay, southwest Newfoundland) hove into view only to be discredited, but fresh discoveries may in due course add new pieces to the jigsaw.

Debate on the subject of the Norse in North America is often fraught, because gaps in the evidence are quickly filled with ingenious narratives, some of which are redolent of the imaginary worlds created by Dan Brown, the Indiana Jones films, and an array of conspiracy theorists. Autodidacts square off against academics, and accusations of insufficient competence and intellectual inflexibility abound. Professionals in the fields of academic enquiry that impinge on the subject rightly grumble about self-appointed experts who have no professional expertise in archaeology, Scandinavian languages and history, manuscripts, cartography, epigraphy, navigation, and science. The public standing of these disciplines, especially those with a scientific dimension, means that amateurs often appropriate the language and deploy the equipment of science without feeling bound by the standards of evidence required by these disciplines—hence the 3D imaging of American runestones and the grid markers on archaeological sites being dug by amateurs. The miming of scientific procedure is not designed to facilitate understanding, as is the case with real science, but to confer scientific credibility on a belief, rather like creation science. Such purposeful endeavours also necessitate a determined amnesia with respect to the accumulated knowledge of a discipline.

In this context it is important that researchers in the field be honest about their expertise and limitations, and I should like to be open about mine. I have some knowledge of the ancient and modern Nordic languages, but am wholly innocent of Kalaallisut (West Greenlandic) and other Inuit languages, of Innu-aimun (Montagnais) and other Algonquian languages, and of Cherokee (Tsalagi) and other Iroquoian languages. In this book I have translated Norse, Danish, Latin, and Spanish as need arose, but included the originals to allow readers the pleasure of detecting shortcomings in my translations. I have hands-on experience of the palaeographical and codicological examination of Latin and vernacular manuscripts. My principal employment in the past decade has been in the museum sector, so I have considerable experience of interpreting genuine artefacts and dealing with fake artefacts and forged manuscripts. My work on classical art and architecture means that I have long been a reader of site reports; I have read many such reports on real and imagined Norse sites, but I am not an archaeologist. I have a working knowledge of the Greek, Hebrew, palaeo-Hebrew, and Coptic scripts sometimes said to appear on American inscriptions, but I am not an epigrapher, and so can comment competently but not authoritatively. My limited command of runes is not based on undergraduate lessons, which I have long forgotten, but rather like that of forgers, derives from a book, in my case my former colleague Martin Findell's excellent little book entitled *Runes* (2014), and an immersion in the learned literature that has given me a sense of the synchronic and diachronic issues—but I am certainly not a runologist. I have an informed interest in cartography, but (despite my great-grandfather's book on *Wrinkles in Practical Navigation*) my command of the history of navigation is limited. Finally, I am a professional student of history, especially literary and cultural history, and am not a scientist, so although

I have some practical experience of the chemistry of ink, in other areas—radiocarbon dating, isotope analysis, pollen analysis, and the history of climate—I am out of my depth, and so can do little more than endeavour to ensure that I am basing my conclusions on the most recent scientific research. This book draws on research in experimental science, social science, and the humanities, and no individual can claim a competent command of all these disciplines. I do, however, know what peer-reviewed research looks like, and have a clear sense of what constitutes evidence and academic consensus.

In 1964 Oxford University Press published Gwyn Jones's *The Norse Atlantic Saga*, of which this book is in some measure a successor. Jones was alert to the possible importance of the excavations being carried out at L'Anse aux Meadows by the Ingstads. By that point it had been established that people who could work iron had lived on the site. 'What awaits a final proof', Jones declared, 'is that they were Norsemen of the early eleventh century'. In the same year that the first edition of the book was published, a soapstone spindle whorl was found on the site, and four years later a ringed bronze pin was found; both were beyond reasonable doubt manufactured by the Norse. The confirmation that the L'Anse aux Meadows site was indeed Norse changed everything. In the words of the UNESCO citation, the site constituted 'a unique milestone in the history of human migration and discovery'. Recognition of the importance of this site has been a spur to the renewal of research, and in the fifty years since the first edition of Professor Jones's book was published, intensive research has expanded both knowledge and understanding.

My first discussion of some of the topics explored in this book was with my former colleague at Liverpool, David Quinn (who believed with good reason that Bristol fishermen were fishing off the north-east coast of America by 1481). Historians attempt to examine and evaluate literary and archaeological evidence with fresh eyes, but inevitably the understanding of evidence is refracted through the prism of published research in the field. In this sense I have incurred intellectual and scholarly debts to many specialists, including Geraldine Barnes, Joel Berglund, Eleanor Rosamund Barraclough, Lisbeth Imer, Christian Keller, Niels Lynnerup, Robert McGhee, Thomas McGovern, Arnved Nedkvitne, Else Østergård, Kirsten Seaver, Patricia Sutherland, Birgitta Wallace, and Henrik Williams. The Norse settlements in Greenland are important for this book, and I should like to acknowledge the huge amount of serious research in the hundreds of volumes of *Meddelelser om Grønland* (Monographs on Greenland), which was established in 1879, and in 1979 was split into three subseries, one of which is *Meddelelser om Grønland, Man & Society*. Historiography is another central concern, and I should like to acknowledge my debt to the work of Reginald Horsman (on racial Anglo-Saxonism), Douglas Hunter (on the Beardmore Relics and Dighton Rock), Annette Kolodny (on myths of first contact), David Krueger (on the Kensington Runestone), and Daniel Woolf (on Stuart historiography). On fake history and archaeological hoaxes, I have profited from the robust polemics of Kenneth Feder and Ronald Fritze.

This book is based on scholarship, but I have written for the wider audience beyond the scholarly community. I have therefore dispensed with footnotes, but have indicated my principal English-language sources in the section on Further Reading. The hegemony of English means that research is increasingly published in that language, but the cutting edge of research is often debated in other languages, in media such as conference papers and blog posts. One example is the question of the origin of the runic symbols on the Kensington Runestone, which as I write (in 2019) is being debated in Swedish on blogs associated with the Swedish National Heritage Board. Eventually most of this research will pass through the peer-review process and be published in English; I have not thought it appropriate to document such work in this book. For similar reasons, I have tried to find a middle ground between popular exonyms and scholarly usage, so I refer to the saga character as Eirik rather than the domesticated Eric/Erik or the scholarly Eiríkr. For the names of other people and peoples (and an explanation of Old Norse terms), see the Glossary. With respect to place names, I use the exonymic forms (usually without accents on vowels) for places named in medieval sources, but retain modern Icelandic spellings for places in Iceland and people in early modern Iceland.

The Old Norse specialist David Clark (University of Leicester) and the ecclesiastical historian Stella Fletcher (University of Warwick) read most or all of an earlier draft, and the archaeologist Patricia Sutherland read the material on Arctic Canada. The two anonymous readers appointed by the Press saved me from some embarrassing inconsistencies in the presentation of sources, and made some very useful suggestions for improving the book, all of which I implemented with gratitude. These readers subsequently waived their anonymity, and I was delighted to discover that they were Eleanor Rosamund Barraclough (Durham University) and Kenneth Feder (Central Connecticut State University); I hold their work in high regard, and now I am in their debt.

For the elucidation of specific points, I am grateful to Gwen Adams (Royal Ontario Museum), Vivian Anderson (Qaqortoq

Museum), Jette Arneborg (National Museum of Denmark), Bruce Bourque (Maine State Museum), Bruce Bradley (University of Exeter), Angelica Duran (Purdue University), Ole Guldager (Narsarsuaq Museum), Christian Koch Madsen (Greenland National Museum and Archives), Jens Christian Moesgaard (National Museum of Denmark), and Lyle Tompsen (Durham University).

At Oxford University Press I worked once again with a highly skilled team, who on this occasion had to work through a pandemic. Matthew Cotton commissioned the book, and Kizzy Taylor-Richelieu oversaw the editorial process. Production was managed by Jayashree Thirumaran of SPi. Cover design was contributed by Scott Greenway, cartography by Phoenix Mapping, copy-editing by Marionne Cronin, and indexing by Geraldine Begley. Marketing was the responsibility of Alison Block, and publicity of Jessica Jones. In New York, Casper Grathwohl secured an important book for me.

My wife Mary travelled with me to most of the sites that I describe, some of which will never be mainstream holiday destinations. She took many of the photographs in this volume, and provided warm companionship in remote places, as she has for many decades.

LEICESTER, 2020 GC

CONTENTS

LIST OF ILLUSTRATIONS

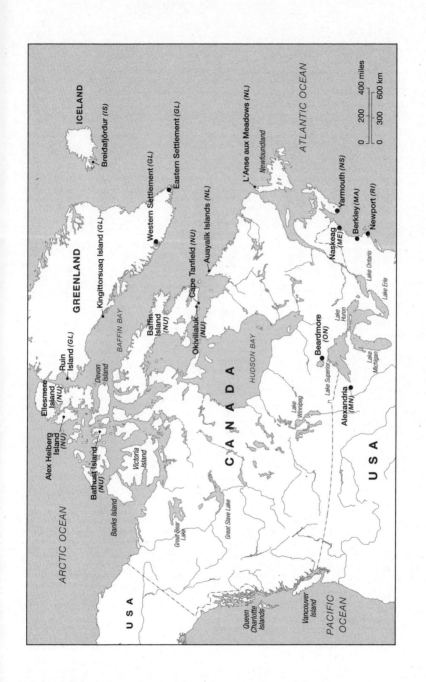

CHAPTER 1

DISCOVERING AMERICA

The imaginations of schoolchildren of my generation were stirred by the stories of Europeans discovering the rest of the world. The greatest figure in these narratives was of course Columbus, who had discovered America. We were entirely untroubled by the fact that the Americas were already populated by the descendants of those who had arrived in America many millennia earlier. In the eyes of the settlers, America was in a sense uninhabited. This language lived on into the twentieth century. Laura Ingalls Wilder's *Little House on the Prairie* (1935) began with a description of the American west as a place where the wild animals wandered free, 'and there were no people. Only Indians lived there'. In 1953 the publisher changed 'people' to 'settlers,' but the novel's depiction of Native Americans and African Americans continues to cause unease in many quarters, as does the affirmation of the white settlers' belief in manifest destiny, the conviction that the European people of the United States were destined and empowered by God to occupy the continent that Columbus had discovered and Providence had allocated to them.

The idea that Columbus discovered America is a relatively recent myth of origin. He is mentioned in historical works of the eighteenth century as the discoverer of America, sometimes in the context of the islands of the Caribbean and sometimes in the broader context of the 'New World'. Those living in the English colonies in America did not speak of discovery, but rather of English origins, and the person who first sailed from England was John Cabot, whose Neapolitan origin as Giovanni Caboto was quietly passed over. The Revolutionary War created a need for colonists to develop an alternative to a founding myth that traced the origins of the United States to England. Columbus, despite the fact that he had never visited what is now the United States, nor even envisaged its existence, was adopted as the discoverer of America.

In 1792, the 300th anniversary of Columbus's first landfall was marked in New York by the Society of St Tammany. In the same year, the historian Jeremy Belknap lifted Columbus out of the reference books with his tercentenary *Discourse intended to commemorate the discovery of America by Christopher Columbus*, which was delivered to the Massachusetts Historical Society on 23 October 1792. The glorification of Columbus was taken in hand by the poet and Jeffersonian politician Joel Barlow, who in 1787 had published by subscription a long poem called *The Vision of Columbus*. The subscribers' list is a roll call of the founding fathers, including George Washington, Benjamin Franklin (6 copies), Thomas Paine, and the Marquis de Lafayette. In 1807 Barlow published an expanded version of the poem in the form of a full-scale epic in the style of Milton's *Paradise Lost*. This new poem, called *The Columbiad*, was intended as a founding epic for America, analogous to Virgil's *Aeneid* as the founding epic of Rome. The poem sets out at tedious length a prophetic vision of the future glories of America (and of a league of all nations); the vision is revealed by an angel to Columbus, who is dying in prison. The poem was enormously popular, and Barlow became the most celebrated poet in the

United States. Columbus was launched. In the land later to become the United States, Columbus is not associated with any particular place, but is simply honoured as the discoverer. He has been thoroughly domesticated, so he is known to Anglophone Americans neither by his name in the dialect of Ligurian spoken in fifteenth-century Genoa (Christoffa Corombo), nor by his name in Spain (Cristóbal Colón), the country that sponsored his voyage, but rather by an anglicized version of his name in Latin, Christophorus Columbus.

After independence the name Columbia was widely adopted as a place name, notably for the capital of South Carolina, the vast river to the Pacific, and the federal district; in 1784, in New York, King's College changed its name to Columbia College. After the War of 1812, there was another burst of place names in honour of Columbus, including the capital of Ohio. In 1892, the 400th anniversary of Columbus's arrival in the Caribbean, President Benjamin Harrison proclaimed the first Columbus Day holiday, which was to honour Columbus as 'the pioneer of progress and enlightenment'. This identification of Columbus with the pioneer spirit also inspired Joaquin Miller's poem 'Columbus' (1892), which was subsequently memorized by generations of American children. In 1882 the order of the Knights of Columbus was founded as a mutual benefit society to aid Catholic families in need; it now has almost two million members. The order was named in honour of Columbus, and its members were instrumental in the campaign to make Columbus Day an annual national celebration. This appropriation of Columbus by American Catholics was to cause unease in some quarters of the Protestant population, and this was one of the factors that led to the emergence of the Viking alternative to Columbus. The difficulty that the Norse were pre-Reformation Catholics was surmounted by treating the eventual conversion of Scandinavia to Protestantism as a retrospective virtue already embedded in the national character of the Norse. Another possible solution to the problem of Columbus being a Catholic Italian was proposed in 1934 by one Thorwald Brynidsen, who argued that Columbus was an American—a Norse resident of the Vinland colony—who had returned to Europe in a Viking ship, changed his name to Cristóbal Colón, and then sailed back to America to rediscover his homeland. This thesis has not enjoyed widespread assent.

The idea that it was the Norse who discovered America first emerged in the late eighteenth century, long before there was any public awareness of the sagas on which such claims were based. In the course of the nineteenth century, evidence for a Norse presence was discovered in what is now the United States. This evidence, in the form of inscriptions and Norse artefacts, generally appeared in areas of Scandinavian settlement, and advocates of the authenticity of this evidence tended to be of Scandinavian descent. Public awareness of the idea of a Norse discovery of America prior to Columbus broadened with the publication by Rasmus Anderson of *America not discovered by Columbus* in 1874. This book lent powerful support both to the historic contention that the Norse visited New England repeatedly from the tenth to the fourteenth centuries and to the Teutonic ancestral link between the Norse and the New England cultural elite known (in the memorable phrase of Oliver Wendell Holmes) as 'the Brahmin caste of New England'.

The high-water mark of the Norse discovery hypothesis came in 1893, three years after the ninth-century Gokstad ship (now in the Viking Ship Museum in Oslo) had been found in a burial mound on Kristianiafjord (now Oslofjord). The quatercentenary of Columbus's first voyage was marked across the United States in 1892, and the following year the World's Columbian Exposition was mounted in Chicago to celebrate Columbus's arrival. It was agreed that the Norwegian contribution would be a reconstruction of the Godstad ship, which would be sailed across the Atlantic (to prove that such a ship was capable of the voyage) to make landfall in New London, Connecticut, and New York before making its way to Chicago, where it would be an exhibit at the exposition. The ship was certainly capable of such a voyage: although it lacked thwarts, it was very strong, and it could be powered by oar or sail. Funding was raised in Norway and from Scandinavians in the United States. On 30 April the *Viking* (as the replica was called) sailed from Bergen under the command of the newspaper publisher Magnus Andersen, and twenty-two days later it reached the shores of America. The American welcome was tumultuous, but not entirely without incident. Anderson's account was published in Norwegian (*Vikingefærden*, i.e. 'Viking expedition') but not in English, and so was never tested against the recollections of Americans who were present; there is no reason to think it unreliable, but it does represent a particular perspective. In this account, Andersen and his crew were attacked in Brooklyn by defenders of Columbus, and the police (Irish Catholics, and so pro-Columbus) treated them as perpetrators rather than victims and held them in the police cells. And as the *Viking* proceeded inland along the Erie Canal to the Great Lakes, the crew was greeted with cries of execration from Columbus enthusiasts on bridges and canal banks. In Anderson's view, this was a confessional divide: Catholics championed Columbus, and Protestants championed the Vikings. This view had already been embedded in popular Protestant culture by writers such as Marie Brown, who in her *The Icelandic Discoverers of America; or Honour to Whom Honour is Due* (1887) had presented the promotion of Columbus's 'fraudulent discovery' as an attempt to make the United States subject to 'the foulest tyrant the world has ever had, the Roman Catholic power'.

The *Viking* was an anomalous presence at an event designed to celebrate Columbus, and it proved to be a cuckoo in the Columbian nest. Anderson and his many supporters stoutly supported the contention that Leif Eirikson had preceded Columbus in America. Indeed, the fact that the *Viking* had sailed the Atlantic without support vessels, whereas the replicas of Columbus's three ships were unseaworthy and so had to be towed across the Atlantic from the Monasterio de La Rábida (the monastery where Columbus stayed while waiting for funding for his voyage), was absorbed into a larger narrative of Scandinavian priority and supremacy. Both narratives are of course mythical—Columbus did not visit what is now the United States, nor is there any evidence that Leif Eirikson did so—but both served ideological purposes. These purposes have been skilfully explored by Annette Kolodny in her very fine book *In Search of First Contact* (2012), and analysed as performative historiography (creating history through re-enactment) in a recent (2017) article by Axel Andersson and Scott Magelssen (see Further Reading). Columbus was important for Catholics, especially Italians and Hispanics. The Vikings were important for both the east-coast elites (which I discuss in chapter 8) and the Scandinavian settlers in the Midwest (discussed in chapter 9 in connection with the Kensington Runestone).

The voyage of the *Viking* supported both fantasy archaeology (it stopped at Newport, Connecticut, home of the 'Viking' Newport Tower) and an ethnic narrative. Commentators were not slow to contrast the manly Norwegians who braved the Atlantic in an open boat with the effeminate Spanish sailors who declined to sail their large vessels across the ocean. The progenitors of New Englanders were deemed to be courageous proto-Protestant Norsemen. This was an appropriation of a similar myth in Britain, memorably articulated by Thomas Carlyle in the first of his lectures in *On heroes, Hero-worship and the Heroic in History*, in which he characterized the 'Sea-Kings' of the 'Northmen' as having 'wild bloody valour' and 'indomitable rugged energy', and lauded their courage, picturing them 'defying the wild ocean with its monsters, and all men and things—progenitors of our own Blakes and Nelsons'. The voyage of the *Viking* encouraged Anglo-Saxon New Englanders and Scandinavian Midwesterners to share in this heroic Nordic ancestry.

The notion that the Vikings had preceded Columbus had widespread support in communities that benefited from this ideological context, but the promotion of Columbus in works such as Washington Irving's hagiographical *Life and Voyages of Christopher Columbus* (1828) also achieved powerful traction in the American historical imagination. Columbus continues to be part of national identity for many Americans, not including Native Americans, who quite sensibly see no reason to celebrate their conquest. Alongside national identity (and again excepting Native Americans), there is a cognate issue with respect to heritage, which may be conceived of geographically or ethnically. Britons are content to see sites such as Skara Brae and Stonehenge as part of their heritage, and there is resistance to the notion that new migrants should be taught about the history of their homelands rather than the history of the British Isles, because heritage is the history of place rather than bloodlines. In North America, the balance is in the other direction. Most Americans do not think of ancient sites such as the pueblos of Chaco Canyon as central to their origins, instead seeking their heritage in South America, Europe, Africa, or Asia. Such a view can be wholly harmless, as in the case of family history, or more malign, as in the case of ethnic history, which too easily slides into racial narratives.

The competing fictions of Columbus and the Vikings are not alone in the field, and there is an important wider context of the question of who discovered America. Many contenders have their advocates, and a consideration of these various claims provides a useful context for understanding the claims for Norse priority that are the central concern of this book. The question of who discovered America is really two questions, the answers to which are often freighted with ideology. First, who were the first human inhabitants of the Americas and how did they get there? Second, who were the first trans-Oceanic visitors to the Americas? Many answers have been given for these questions, and the evidence adduced for various candidates includes both fanciful interpretations of archaeological sites and artefacts that have been faked. Understanding the contexts of such spurious evidence is a useful preliminary to understanding the claims made for a Norse presence in America that will be the subject of the closing chapters of this book.

On the first question, that of the first human inhabitants of the Americas, there was once a scholarly consensus that was virtually unchallenged, and trickled down into the history lessons of my childhood. The Indians, as they were then called, had come from Siberia, crossed on the Beringia land bridge that extended across what is now the Bering Strait, and then travelled south through the ice-free corridor that, as the glaciers retreated, had opened up between the vast ice sheets that covered Canada. The corridor (through what is now Alberta) provided pasturage and passage for the animals—including bison, mammoths, and horses—to the plains of America, and the Siberian hunters followed in their wake. These pioneers reached what is now the United States at the end of the last ice age. In the 1920s and 1930s, excavations near the town of Clovis, in eastern New Mexico, revealed Pleistocene animals and distinctive tools carved from bone and ivory. The people that hunted these animals and produced these tools became known as the Clovis culture. The perfectly sensible hypothesis that the Clovis people were the first human inhabitants of the Americas hardened into the fact of 'Clovis First'. In recent years, however, this contention has been challenged and subverted by the discovery of pre-Clovis cultures in the Americas.

Such discoveries create a problem, in that the dating of the pre-Clovis cultures means that these peoples arrived in the Americas before the ice-free corridor could have opened up. There is an additional difficulty in the lack of archaeological evidence for such a corridor, the existence of which is sustained by the need for a route that early migrants could travel. In short, the Clovis First hypothesis has been discredited, but no consensus has formed around an alternative hypothesis. Some argue that migration was along the north Pacific Rim in small boats. A beleaguered minority of academic prehistorians has explored the possibility that Solutrean people of south-west Europe may have crossed on a North Atlantic ice bridge. Real science is cautious in its conclusions, because of an insistence that conclusions be evidence-based. When there are gaps in the evidence, amateurs rush in with narratives that can fill in the gaps. These narratives, and the ideologies that drive them, are a central concern of this book. In the case of the United States, they provide a context for the popular thinking about Vikings that is a central strand in this book.

The scientific community is united in its conviction that the earliest inhabitants of North America, who migrated by unknown means and routes from other continents, were the remote ancestors of today's indigenous North Americans. Some indigenous North Americans resist the notion of migration, holding fast to the traditional belief that their ancestors were created in the land that they now occupy. This is one of a number of beliefs about early America arising from religious or cultural conviction. Another example is the account in the Book of Mormon, which records that four groups (Jaredites, Nephites, Lamanites and Mulekites) migrated to America in remote antiquity, either after the fragmentation of human language as a consequence of the construction of the Tower of Babel, or after the destruction of Solomon's temple in Jerusalem in 587 BCE. Early Mormons believed that Native Americans were the descendants of these early migrants, and some still adhere to this belief.

Religious convictions have coloured convictions about the origin of Native Americans since the colonial period. Cotton Mather, the prolific (380 titles) and pedantic voice of Puritan America, declared in his sermon *The Serviceable Man* (delivered 28 March 1690) that

> 'Tis probable, that a large part of the *Americans* are the Posterity of those *Canaanites*, who after the Wars of *Canaan*, did set up their Pillars in *Africa*, with that Inscription on them, *We are of those that Fled from the Face of Joshua the Robber*.

The allusion is to a story in Procopius about two pillars of stone near Tangier, inscribed in Phoenician with the words that Mather quotes. From Tangier, the Canaanites moved to America. As for the Puritan colonists, Mather declares that 'Tis the prerogative of *New-England* above all the Countries of the world, *That it is a Plantation for the Christian and Protestant Religion*'. He concludes that you may see 'an *Israel* in *America*, by looking upon this Plantation; may *Peace be upon this Israel of God!*'

The Indian Wars are thus presented as a righteous re-enactment of the invasion of Canaan by the people of Israel. The unambiguous commands of the God of Israel to 'save alive nothing that breathes' in the Canaanite cities justified the killing of men, women, children, and livestock, and in the 'Israel in America' proclaimed by Mather, such brutality was justified by divine command. Thus, in 1637 a godly band surrounded and torched a Pequot village in Connecticut, incinerating men, women, and children. William Bradford, the governor of Plymouth Colony, wrote in his *History of Plymouth Plantation*

> Those that scaped the fire were slain with the sword; some hewed to pieces, other run through with their rapiers, so as they were quickly dispatched, and very few escaped. It was conceived they thus destroyed about 400, at this time. It was a fearful sight to see them thus frying in the fire, and the streams of blood quenching the same, and horrible was the stink and scent thereof; but the victory seemed a sweet sacrifice, and they gave the prayers thereof to God, who had wrought so wonderfully for them, thus to enclose their enemies in their hands, and give them so speedy a victory over so proud and insulting an enemy.

John Mason, the commanding officer of the massacre, later wrote that the attack was the work of a God 'who laughed his enemies and the enemies of his people to scorn, making them as a fiery oven'. The dark underside of manifest destiny is genocide.

Cotton Mather thought that Native Americans were the descendants of Canaanites, but some of his contemporaries took the view that they were the descendants of Jews. One early champion of the idea that America was the refuge of the ten lost tribes of Israel was Thomas Thorowgood, who set out his arguments in *Jewes in America or Probabilities that the Americans are of that Race* (1650). Thorowgood's arguments were sufficiently familiar to his American contemporaries for Cotton Mather to claim in his memoir of John Eliot, the translator of the Bible into an Algonquian language, that Eliot had 'Thorow-good reasons' for his mistaken belief that Native Americans were descended from the lost tribes of Israel. There was even support for the lost tribes hypothesis from the learned Portuguese rabbi Menasseh ben Israel, who prefaced his *Hope of Israel* (translated into English in 1651) with the story of Antonio de Montezinos, a Marrano Jew who had found one of the lost tribes in Ecuador. Menasseh agreed with Montezinos 'that the first inhabitants of America were the Ten Tribes of the Israelites'. The ten lost tribes hypothesis has enjoyed continuous support since the seventeenth century. Proponents included Elias Boudinot, president of the Continental Congress, who in 1816 published *A star in the west, or, A humble attempt to discover the long lost ten tribes of Israel: preparatory to their return to their beloved city, Jerusalem.*

In due course, archaeological evidence for the early presence of Jews in America emerged. The Newark Holy Stones, now on display in the Johnson-Humrickhouse Museum in Coshocton, Ohio, were discovered several months apart in 1860, in the midst of Native American burial mounds. The first to be discovered, a sandstone shaped like a keystone, has four Hebrew phrases ('the

Holy of Holies', 'the King of the Earth', 'the Law of God', and 'the Word of the Lord'), carved in the distinctive form of the square script (influenced by Aramaic) that emerged after the Babylonian Exile. This discovery vindicated the theory that the first Americans were Jews, but there was a competing explanation: the keystone was identified as Masonic, and so constituted evidence that ancient Masons had constructed the earthworks. There were reservations, however: the dispersal of the ten tribes had occurred long before the Exile, and so the relative modernity of the script was problematical.

Several months later, a second stone was found nearby, this time written in a palaeo-Hebraic script in use before the Exile. This stone has a condensed transcription of the Ten Commandments in the version found in Exodus 20, and so is known as the Decalogue Stone. The inscription encompasses a low-relief carving of a man identified in the Hebrew caption as Moses. This discovery invalidated the Masonic hypothesis, but lent powerful support to the theory of Jewish origins. It has been variously interpreted as an ancient arm phylactery (Hebrew: *tefillah*) of the Second Temple period, or a Samaritan mezuzah (which, unlike its Jewish equivalent, was typically a large stone on which the Decalogue was inscribed). Most of the Hebrew lettering exhibits a modest competence, but several letters give me pause. The versions of *alef, ayin, mem,* and *yod* could be variants unknown to me, but to my eye they resemble Greek or Coptic more than Hebrew. The version of Hebrew *sadhe* in the inscriptions simply puzzles me, as does the appearance of a terminal *kaph* where one expects a *daleth* (in the verb 'to covet'); the letters are certainly similar in modern Hebrew, but not in palaeo-Hebrew. Such evidence points to the likelihood that the inscription was copied from a printed Hebrew text. The hypothesis of a Samaritan mezuzah is equally highly unlikely: the Samaritan Decalogue compresses the commandments to accommodate an extra commandment ordering the construction of a temple on Mount Gerizim, yet this stone presents a Hebrew Decalogue.

It seems reasonable to conclude that the Newark Holy Stones were incised in the nineteenth century. Bradley Lepper and Jeff Gill, the principal scholarly students of the stones, argue that the only local person with the requisite command of Hebrew was John McCarty, the Episcopalian priest who had translated both the stones, so he must be the primary suspect. His bishop, Charles McIlvaine, had a learned interest in early Christian antiquities in America. He was also a combatant in the culture war over the issue of slavery, believing that all humans had descended from Adam and Eve (the doctrine of monogenesis) and that human slavery was utterly unacceptable. He was therefore an opponent of the view that separate races were separate species and that slavery was therefore consistent with the will of God. One prominent proponent of this latter view (the doctrine of polygenesis) was Josiah Nott, who had argued that the antiquity of the mounds meant that they must be pre-Adamic, and that the Biblical account must be erroneous. The discovery of the Newark Holy Stones showed that Nott was wrong, that the mounds were not just post-Adamic, but post-Mosaic. The priest had therefore gifted his bishop with evidence that supported his bishop's position in the debate. But perhaps this is a coincidence.

The Los Lunas Decalogue Stone was found in New Mexico in 1933. The text is inscribed on the flat surface of an 80-ton boulder, and so it has never been moved to a museum. In 2006 it was vandalized, and the first line of the inscription has been chipped away.

Like the Newark Decalogue Stone, it contains an abbreviated version of the Ten Commandments, written in a palaeo-Hebrew script that could be Samaritan or Moabite. There is also, as in the Newark Stone, the odd phenomenon of Greek letters standing in for palaeo-Hebrew, so the Hebrew *dalet*, *zayin*, and *taw* are represented by the Greek letters *delta*, *zeta*, and *tau*. It seems odd to have Greek letters in a Hebrew text, even a Hellenistic one. The lettering appears to have been incised with modern tools, and the site offers no archaeological context. The evidence points to the Los Lunas Stone being another modern creation.The Bat Creek Stone, now on long-term loan from the Smithsonian Institution to the Museum of the Cherokee Indian in North Carolina, was found in 1889 in an apparently undisturbed burial mound by a member of the Smithsonian's Mound Survey Project. The letters were confidently identified as deriving from a pre-Columbian Cherokee syllabary, a predecessor to the syllabary developed in the early nineteenth century by a Cherokee called Sequoyah. No one has attempted a translation. In 1964 Henriette Mertz, who believed that America had been discovered by Odysseus from the east and Chinese travellers from the west, noticed that if the Bat Creek Stone were inverted, what was apparently Cherokee became Phoenician, and so argued it should be considered alongside artefacts such as the Phoenician inscription on the Grave Creek Stone in West Virginia. This observation was soon refined by Cyrus Gordon (a prominent proponent of pre-Columbian contact), and the inscription was said to be palaeo-Hebrew from the first or second centuries CE. This is a problematical dating because palaeo-Hebrew was, except for coinage and a few instances in early Dead Sea Scrolls, obsolete by the first or second centuries CE. The exact meaning of the inscription is unclear, but it seems to centre on the word 'Judea'. In 2004, the archaeologists Robert Mainfort and Mary Kwas argued convincingly that the inscription was inexpertly copied from a Masonic reference book published in 1870. Others have argued that the script is not Hebrew, but Coelbren, the ancient Welsh alphabet, and that it says 'Madoc the ruler he is', and so have inferred that the mound is the tomb of Madoc, of whom more below. One difficulty with this reading is that Coelbren y Beirdd ('the bard's alphabet') is not ancient but a nineteenth-century invention by the Welsh forger Edward Williams.

Many such inscriptions have been found in the United States. The tablets unearthed in Davenport, Iowa, by a Lutheran pastor in 1877 contain incomprehensible glyphs and what appears to be a depiction of human sacrifice. The Smithsonian took the tablets seriously, but its confidence dwindled when it was discovered that the tablets were roof tiles from a local brothel. Similarly, the Michigan relics, a cache of inscribed artefacts discovered in 1890 by a local sign painter in Edmore, Michigan, expanded into thousands of objects in the course of the next twenty years. The finds included tablets in ancient scripts, some depicting Biblical scenes. Those taking an interest included a prominent Mormon scientist, who concluded that the artefacts were frauds, but one of his co-religionists, Rudolph Etzenhauer, published a book in which he argued that the relics vindicated the historicity of the Book of Mormon. In 2003 the Church History Museum in Salt Lake City donated its collection of almost 800 Michigan Relics to the Michigan History Museum in Lancing.

The idea that Native Americans were preceded by other civilizations was sometimes prompted by the large mounds that dot the American landscape, most conspicuously in the Mississippi River valley and the Ohio River valley. Perhaps the best known are the Cahokia Mounds in Illinois, which now enjoy UNESCO World Heritage status. The most substantial mound on the site, Monks Mound, is the largest pre-Columbian earthwork in North America. The demeaning view of Native Americans shared by many settlers in America led them to believe that construction of the mounds would have exceeded the capabilities of Native Americans and must therefore have been the work of a superior previous civilization. Benjamin Smith Barton, a distinguished physician and naturalist, proposed in 1787 that Vikings had built the mounds; ten years later he revised his view and attributed them to Native Americans. In 1876 the Greek-American Lafcadio Hearn attributed them to refugees from the sunken island of Atlantis. Others championed European or Chinese groups as the builders. Members of the Moorish Science Temple of America, who claim Moorish origins for African-Americans, declare on their website that the Mound Builders, who had an advanced knowledge of cosmic forces, migrated from Mexico after Atlantis was sunk. This tide of fantasy overwhelmed early scholarly enquiry, which had begun with Thomas Jefferson's careful excavation of a mound near his property. He found many skeletons, but drew no conclusions, instead encouraging members of the American Philosophical Society (of which he was president) to conduct a scholarly investigation into the identity of the Mound Builders.

The debate about the identity of the Mound Builders should not be dismissed as harmless nonsense, because it is pernicious nonsense: it turns the victims of violent conquest into its perpetrators. Defending the 'benevolent' Indian Removal Act of 1830, Andrew Jackson told Congress that it would 'place a dense and civilized population in large tracts of country now occupied by a few savage hunters'. The Act explains that true philanthropy reconciles the mind 'to the extinction of one generation to make room for another', and just as the Act is extinguishing the Indians from areas of white settlement, so the Indians extinguished the mound-building civilization that preceded theirs: 'In the monuments and fortresses of an unknown people, spread over the extensive regions of the West, we behold the memorials of a once powerful race, which was exterminated or has disappeared to make room for the existing savage tribes'.

The theory of a sophisticated vanished race of Mound Builders that preceded the arrival of Native Americans was a commonplace among Americans of European descent in the late eighteenth and nineteenth centuries. It has now faded from public debate and has become the preserve of enthusiasts. I recently (2018) visited the mounds in Natchez, Mississippi, which are responsibly presented as Native American mounds. I was assured by a member of staff that they are periodically informed by visitors that the Vikings built the mounds.

The notion of discovery prior to the arrival of Native Americans flared up again with the discovery of the prehistoric skeleton of Kennewick Man in the state of Washington in 1996. Members of the Umatilla nation demanded that the bones be handed over to them for reburial, but their claim was resisted pending the outcome of a scientific enquiry. In the ensuing investigation of the ancestry and ethic affiliations of the skeleton, the bones were said to be Caucasoid rather than Native American, and were carbon-dated to c. 7400 BCE. This conclusion was merely puzzling, but was soon turned to sinister use by a group called the Asatru Folk Assembly, which lodged a rival claim to the bones. This Assembly is not the wholly benign new religious movement known as Ásatrú ('allegiance to the gods'), founded in Iceland in 1972 with a view to reviving the polytheistic traditions of Iceland's pre-Christian past, but rather a white supremacist offshoot founded in California in 1994; its URL hostname is 'runestone'. In the view of the Asatru Folk Assembly, Kennewick Man vindicated the claim that Europeans enjoyed the legitimacy of first settlement and that Native Americans were subsequent migrants.

Scientists wanted to investigate further, so there were then three claimants to the bones: the Umatilla, the Asatru Folk Assembly, and a group of anthropologists acting on behalf of the scientific community. The Army Corps, which owned the land, impounded the bones, and a protracted legal battle ensued. The case slowly rose through the courts, and in 2004 the Court of Appeals ruled in favour of the scientists. In 2014 the scientific community, represented by sixty-five scientists, published a massive (680 pages) account of the scientific investigation (see Owsley, 2014, in Further Reading), concluding that Kennewick Man's genetic lineage can safely be associated with modern Native Americans now living in the area where he was found. A subsequent independent investigation led by Danish scientists (see Rasmussen, 2015, in Further Reading) concluded that the Kennewick Man could not be associated with any contemporary group, but was certainly of native North American descent. The early claims for his European ancestry, however, are a reminder than many debates about first arrivals are rooted in ideologies of race and ethnicity.

In the nineteenth century, mysterious inscriptions and petroglyphs led to a vogue for the view that the Americas had first been settled by Phoenicians. Traces of tobacco in Egyptian mummies (noted by their cigarette-smoking excavators) were believed by some to indicate that Egyptians had crossed the Atlantic. Clay storage pots found in Brazil have convinced others that the Romans had visited America. The similarities between the art of the Olmecs in Mexico and that of sub-Saharan African have led others to claim that it was Africans who discovered America.

What these claims to the peopling of America have in common is ethnic pride, sometimes accompanied by an attempt to discredit the claim of native Americans to be the founding peoples of America. The descendants of Europeans who took the land of native Americans and then drove them to the verge of extinction are reluctant to yield to them the honour of a prior claim to America.

The question of the identity of the first human inhabitants of the Americas is tied by ideology to the related question of the identity of the first trans-Oceanic visitors to the Americas. The story of Columbus is the principal but not the only narrative, because there has long been an awareness that Norse seafarers had discovered Greenland and established settlements there that lasted for centuries. Despite the fact that at one point Greenland is separated from Canada by a shallow channel only 16 miles (26 km) across, Greenland was thought of as part of Europe, a notion reinforced by the fact that it was a Danish possession. The Norse discovery of Greenland did not dislodge Columbus as the person who had discovered America, but it became the principal competitor to the Columbian hypothesis.

The primacy of Columbus has been challenged for centuries. In 1507 the German cartographer Martin Waldseemüller proposed that the new continent should be called 'America, because Americus discovered it'. This misguided attribution of the European discovery of America to the Florentine Amerigo Vespucci did ensure that his name would be forever preserved, but occluded Amerigo's real achievement, which was to be the first European to understand that what Columbus had discovered was indeed a continent unknown to Europeans and not, as Columbus insisted, a remote part of Asia.

There have been many other claimants to the crown of Columbus. The Irish claim centres on St Brendan, who in the sixth century sailed to America in his coracle; his descendants now populate Boston. The Scottish claimant is Henry Sinclair, earl of Orkney, who reached Greenland and the North American continent in the fourteenth century. A member of his expedition is said to be commemorated in the image of the 'Westford Knight' inscribed on Sinclair Rock, in Westford, Massachusetts; the image was first identified in Frederick Pohl's *Prince Henry Sinclair: His expedition to the New World in 1398* (1972). The Welsh claimant is Madog ab Owain Gwynedd, who landed on the Atlantic coast of America. Madog's precedence is actively promoted in both America and Wales. Several cities, notably Mobile, Alabama (on the Gulf of Mexico), vie for the honour of being Madog's point of landfall, and in 1953 the Mobile chapter of the Daughters of the American Revolution erected a plaque at Fort Morgan 'in memory of Prince Madoc a Welsh explorer who landed on the shores of Mobile Bay in 1170 and left behind, with the Indians, the Welsh language'; the plaque was removed by Parks officials in 2008. A similar plaque at Madog's port of embarkation could still be seen in 2017 in a rockery at a house called Odstone, in Rhos-on-Sea: 'Prince Madoc sailed from here Aber Kerrik Gwynan 1170 AD and landed at Mobile, Alabama with his ships Gorn Gwynant and Pedr Sant'. Odstone was demolished on September 2017, and as I write, the plaque has been temporarily removed, but plans are afoot for the celebration of the 850th anniversary of the voyage in 2020.

The historicity of Madog's voyage is compromised by the ontological problem that he never existed (Owain Gwynedd, who is the well-documented king of Gwynedd, did not have a son called Madog), but the legend served a purpose. Wales had been conquered by Edward I in the late thirteenth century and was a principality annexed to the English crown until 1536, when it was incorporated into England (though the principality lives on in the anachronistic title 'Prince of Wales'). That meant that Madog's American expeditions stood as proxy for the English claim to have reached America before Columbus. The story exists in many variants, but one important strand has Madog and his settlers moving north from Mobile Bay. En route they built fortifications such as the Old Stone Fort in Tennessee (later claimed to be a Viking structure). Survivors of the journey settled in the Dakotas, where they became the Mandan tribe. Many travellers testified to the existence of Welsh-speaking Indians. Francis Lewis, a Welsh-born signatory of the Declaration of Independence, claimed to have been captured by Indians, and escaped being tied to a stake and burnt alive when he addressed his captors in Welsh and was relieved to discover that they understood him.

In the wake of the Nootka Crisis of 1789, in which Spain laid claim to British possessions, the legend of Madog was revitalized, and in 1796–7 the Welsh explorer John Thomas Evans, acting for Spain, lived amongst the Mandan for six months. He found no Welsh speakers, and his report (published in the American and Welsh press) concluded that 'there is no such people as the Welsh Indians'. This conclusion was naturally unacceptable to believers in Welsh Indians, who assumed that the perfidious Spaniards had either altered his report or paid him to falsify his findings. Belief in

Madog and the Welsh Indians has lived on. In the mid twentieth century, Zella Armstrong published *Who Discovered America? The amazing story of Madoc* (1950). In the twentieth-first century, there is an active Madoc International Research Association (based in Wales). In America, one Ken Lonewolf identifies as the last 'wisdom-keeper' of the Shawnee-White Madoc Native Americans.

The principal Western proponent of the view that the Chinese reached America before Columbus is Gavin Menzies, who in two books (1421: *The Year China Discovered the World*, 2002; *Who Discovered America*, 2013) has elaborated his contention that a map dated 1418 demonstrated that a Chinese admiral, Zheng He, had sailed his great fleet of junks round the world and visited the Americas a century before Columbus. Zheng He is also said to have circumnavigated Greenland, pausing en route to sail up a fjord in the Eastern Settlement to Hvalsey, where the fleet's presence is said to be attested by DNA analysis which has 'shown that the native people around Hvalsey possess Chinese DNA'. The reception of such claims attests to the unhappy divide between academic historians, who rightly denounce Menzies' work as fantasy, and in turn are denounced as so-called experts. Gavin Menzies has said 'the public are on my side, and they are the people who count'. Commercial success is not a measure of historical probity, so in the absence of credible evidence, the story of Zheng He's voyage must be regarded as very readable historical fiction.

In 2014, Turkish President Recep Erdogan announced that Muslim sailors had reached the Americas in 1178, more than 300 years before Columbus, adducing Columbus's observation that he had seen what looked like a mosque on a hilltop in Cuba. He ordered that this discovery be embedded in the history syllabus in all Turkish schools. The ruins of mosques and inscriptions from the Qur'an are also said to have been discovered in Texas and Nevada.

Barry Fell, of whom more below, discovered evidence of an extensive system of Islamic schools in the writing and diagrams etched in the rocks at many sites in Nevada (Allen Springs, Hickison Summit, Keyhole Canyon, Lagomarsino, Valley of Fire, and Washoe County) and in sites in Colorado (Mesa Verde), New Mexico (Mimbres Valley), and Indiana (Tippecanoe County). These petroglyphs are usually understood as Native American art, but Fell argued that they were Kufic script (the earliest form of Arabic writing), that the language was North African Arabic, that the educational subjects indicated by the inscriptions ranged from mathematics and astronomy to history, geography, and navigation by sea, and that they could be dated to the eighth century. Finally, he argued that the descendants of these Muslim settlers were the ancient groups known as Olmec, Anasazi, and Hohokam, and the living Native Americans and First Nations Canadians of the Algonquian and Iroquois peoples.

The claim that Africans preceded Europeans in America was memorably championed by Leo Weiner in his *Africa and the Discovery of America* (3 volumes, 1920–2). Weiner argued that the Mandinka people of West Africa had migrated to Mexico and thence spread throughout the Americas. In North America, they are said to have traded and intermarried with both Algonquian and Iroquois Indians. And, as the Mandinka were predominantly Muslim, Weiner's theories have been adopted by those who want Muslims to have preceded Christians in America.

Evidence for such claims is often explored by opponents of the Columbian narrative. One such anti-Columbian was Barry

Fell, a distinguished invertebrate zoologist at Harvard's Museum of Comparative Zoology. Fell was a self-taught epigrapher, who published three books (*America BC*, 1976; *Saga America*, 1980; *Bronze Age America*, 1982) on American inscriptions, demonstrating to his own satisfaction inscriptional evidence for the presence of groups such as Basques, Celts, Egyptians, and Phoenicians in America centuries before Columbus. He interpreted the markings on the Bourne Stone in Massachusetts, for example, as an Iberian script proclaiming the annexation of the site by a prehistoric Spaniard. Spoilsport archaeologists interpret the stone as the doorstep of a seventeenth-century Native American meetinghouse.

Such claims are routinely dismissed by archaeologists and historians, but that does not cool the passion of their proponents. The notion of Norse discovery is similarly freighted with ideology and ethnic self-interest, but at least there is evidence of contact. This book is not, however, simply an account of the Norse discovery of America presented in competition with other such claims. It is in part an account of Norse expansion to the west, which completed the human encircling of the globe. However they arrived, humans spread through the Americas, and eventually, in recorded history, Norse people on the edge of Europe made contact with people on the edge of North America, thus closing the circle of humanity. The first part of this book is an account of that process. My focus is on the Europeans whose journeys closed the circle, but I am conscious that it was the ancestors of the autochthonous peoples of the Americas who had walked the furthest, and that the Norse had travelled a comparatively short distance to America while remaining seated in their ships.

My second purpose is to explore what happens when those who want their ancestors to be the Nordic discoverers of the already-discovered Americas are faced with a lack of evidence. A scholarly truism has it that absence of evidence is not evidence of absence, but the problem has all too often been addressed by manufactured evidence that is trusted by those keen to believe it. This story could be construed as an account of credulity and fraud, but, perhaps more importantly, it is an assertion of a narrative grounded in a sense of racial superiority fortified by exceptionalism.

The cultural context of the Viking revival lies in assumptions about race that are now rightly regarded as repugnant. As Reginald Horsman argued in his *Race and Manifest Destiny: The origins of American Racial Anglo-Saxonism* (1986), in the second half of the nineteenth century American expansionism was not viewed so much as a vindication of democratic republicanism as of 'evidence of the innate superiority of the American Anglo-Saxon branch of the Caucasian race'. Columbus could not have been the first to discover America, because he was an Italian working in the service of Spain. On this reading, America was discovered by Vikings.

In this book I have used the term 'Norse' to denote the medieval peoples of Scandinavia, and 'Vikings' to denote the imaginary race invented in the nineteenth century (sometimes called 'Northmen'). In Old Norse '*vikingr*' may have meant something like 'raider' or 'pirate'. The term first appeared in modern English in 1807 (spelt 'vikingr'), and first appeared in the familiar modern spelling in Longfellow's 'Skeleton in Armor' ('I was a Viking old'). In the second half of the nineteenth century, horned and winged helmets became the distinguishing feature of these Vikings of the imagination, all of whom were of course male. As Charles Kingsley said in a letter of 1849, the Anglo-Saxons, 'a female race', 'required impregnation by the great male race' of Northmen. The Norse wore helmets when conducting raids, but the helmets were smooth so that they would deflect a sword blow; a horned helmet would catch a sword blade, and allow the helmet (and the head) to be removed. Viking helmets first acquired horns in book illustrations of the Norse sagas, such as the English edition of the Saga of Frithiof published in 1839. Paintings of Norse raiders by the Swedish artist Johan August Malmström in the 1850s took up the theme. Horned helmets were popularized by Carl Emil Doepler, who in the 1870s designed the costumes for Wagner's Ring cycle, and equipped the Nordic characters with horned helmets. Thereafter horned or winged helmets became obligatory headgear for Vikings, so in the huge statue of a Viking in Alexandria, Minnesota (see Fig. 9.3), his helmet is winged.

I shall return to the imaginary Viking in my final chapters. In the early chapters, I shall track the saga of the Norse across the North Atlantic to America. The journey that I describe is a continuum, with evidence-based history and archaeology at one end, and fake history and outright fraud at the other. In between there lies a huge expanse of uncertainty: sagas that may contain shards of truth, characters that may be partly historical, real archaeology that may be interpreted through the fictions of saga, and fragmentary evidence open to responsible and irresponsible interpretation. There are, therefore, two narratives in the chapters that follow. The first is the westward expansion of the Norse across the North Atlantic, ending (but not culminating) in a fleeting and ill-documented presence on the shores of the North American mainland. The second is the appropriation and enhancement of the westward narrative by Canadians and Americans who want the Vikings to have discovered America, and in the advancement of that thesis have been willing to manufacture fake evidence in support of claims grounded in an ideology of racial superiority.

CHAPTER 2

SAGAS AND CHRONICLES

The Icelandic sagas are an important strand in a large and distinguished corpus of narrative compositions from medieval Iceland and Norway. These sagas purport to record the history of the Norse and Celtic inhabitants of Iceland from the first settlements, in the late ninth century. The narratives originated in the oral tradition of storytelling, passing from generation to generation, until they were finally written down in the thirteenth and fourteenth centuries. At some point a variety of written sources began to supplement the material from the oral tradition. It is difficult to know precisely when this happened, because the transmission history from the earliest written accounts (none of which survive) to the earliest surviving manuscripts is unknown. In these respects, the Icelandic sagas are comparable to the primary epics of classical antiquity. The *Iliad*, for example, describes events said to have occurred in c. 1200 BCE, but it seems not to have been written until c. 750 BCE, and the earliest surviving textual fragment (on a clay tablet discovered in 2018) is from the third century CE. On the contentious question of historicity, the attitudes that inform the archaeology of Troy provide an instructive analogy for understanding the sagas.

A site called Hisarlık, a few miles from the western coast of Anatolia (now Turkey), has long been assumed to be Homer's

Troy. There have been three periods of excavation. The first dig (1870–90) was the work of Heinrich Schliemann, who was determined to prove that the *Iliad* was the record of an historical conflict in which the major protagonists were those described by Homer. His excavation had a strong emphasis on artefacts, so a haul of almost 9,000 pieces was triumphantly declared to be Priam's Treasure, and the level known as Troy II was identified as the Homeric city. The second dig (1932–38) was led by Carl Blegen (elder brother of Theodore Blegen, author of a book on the Kensington Runestone), who was more interested in stratigraphy than treasure hunting. Blegen identified Troy VIIA to be the city of the Trojan War, which he believed to be historical. The third dig, an examination of the Bronze Age strata, was led by Manfred Korfmann from 1981 until his death in 2005. His excavation was not undertaken with a view to understanding the *Iliad* or the Trojan War, but rather to explore the significance of the site for an understanding of the Late Bronze Age. He took the view that the archaeological record implies the existence of armed conflicts in the area c. 1200 BCE, but that there is no archaeological evidence for or against the contention that there was a single episode that might be described as the Trojan War. On this reading, the *Iliad* may preserve remnants of the memory of a Greek attack on the Anatolian coast. Such fragments of memory may transmit elements of place, but are unlikely to transmit names and actions of individuals. Scholarship has moved away from what is termed euhemerism, which is the practice of treating mythical accounts as if they were records of real people and events.

The sagas that describe journeys are a parallel case, in that they are often treated as if they were logbooks recording actual voyages by the named historical individuals. It is not safe to assume this to be the case. There may have been a chieftain called Eirik the Red around whom legends accumulated, and it is possible that he had a son called Leif Eirikson. Their voyages to Greenland and then lands to the west of Greenland, as described in the sagas, may never have happened. It is of course possible that these characters did exist and that the sagas preserve shards of memory. In other words, Eirik and Leif and their companions exist in the liminal space between fact and fiction.

To assert that these characters are borderline historical figures is therefore not to deny that the Norse settled in Greenland in the late tenth century (a date confirmed by radiocarbon analysis) and travelled to the North American mainland, but rather to caution against using archaeology as a mechanism for confirming the truth of the sagas, as Schliemann did at Hisarlık. I do not, therefore, assume that any congruity between a saga and the archaeology of a site confirms the truthfulness of an episode in the saga. One example would be Brattahlid, Eirik's farm in the Eastern Settlement of Greenland, where his wife Thjodhild is said to have built a church. The site of Eirik's farm is usually (but not always) identified as what is now the village of Qassiarsuk, which has the foundations of a late tenth-century church now known as Thjodhild's Church. A modern statue of Leif Eirikson looms over the village, the initiative of the Leif Erikson International Foundation in Seattle, Washington. At the unveiling ceremony in 2000, the Norwegian Ladies Chorus of Seattle welcomed the arrival of the statue in song. Thus a character from the sagas was transformed into a solidly historical figure and appropriated in an act of public history by Scandinavian Americans asserting their priority in America.

There are two sagas, *Saga of the Greenlanders* and *Saga of Eirik the Red* (together known as the Vinland Sagas), that contain full accounts of Greenland and the lands to the west. Both describe voyages in the late tenth and early eleventh centuries. The earliest versions were probably composed in the twelfth century and were transmitted orally until written down in the thirteenth century. The purpose of these sagas was not to describe the events of the expansion to the west, even though these accounts are central to the narrative. Their genre is that of family saga, and they were composed to honour illustrious forebears. There is an analogy in Shakespeare's *Macbeth*, where the character of Banquo is given a dynastic role because King James I, in whose reign the play was written, believed that Banquo was one of his ancestors. As it happens, Banquo never existed (he was invented by Hector Boece, a Scottish chronicler, in the early sixteenth century), but in the view of King James and his Scottish contemporaries, he was an important historical figure.

So it is with the Vinland Sagas. In the twelfth century the church had two dioceses in Iceland, and their episcopal seats were at Skálholt and Hólar. In the early twelfth century the bishop of Skálholt was Thorlak Runolfsson (1118–1133). In the mid twelfth century, the bishop of Hólar was Björn Gilsson (1147–1162), who was succeeded by Brand Saemundsson (1163–1201). All three bishops are named at the conclusion of both Vinland Sagas as descendants of Thorfinn Karlsefni and his Christian wife, Gudrid Thorbjarnardottir. Just as Shakespeare flatters the King with an account of his heroic ancestors Banquo and Fleance, so the writers of the sagas flatter the bishops with accounts of their heroic great-grandfathers (and in Bishop Brand's case, great-great-grandfather) and their pious great- (or great-great-) grandmother. In the case of Björn Gilsson, there may be a particular reason for the glorification of his ancestors. In the twelfth century there was a proposal to prepare a 'cause' for the canonization of Bishop Björn. Heroic ancestors would constitute part of the case, and the *Saga of Eirik the Red* may well have been envisaged as a contribution to the cause.

In both *Macbeth* and the sagas, the prophecies of distinguished descendants reach down to the future. In *Macbeth* the Third Witch tells Banquo that his descendants will be kings ('thou shall get kings'), and there is a 'show of eight kings' representing the succession of the Stuarts down to King James (the ninth Stuart). In the *Saga of Eirik the Red*, there is a similar passage, in which the prophet Thorbjörg says of Gudrid,

> You will make a good marriage here in Greenland, but it will be short-lived, because your path will lead you to Iceland, where you will be the mother of a great family line, over whom will shine a bright light
>
> [Þú munt gjaforð fá hér á Grænlandi, þat er sæmiligast er, þó at þér verði þat eigi til langæðar, því at vegir þínir liggja út til Íslands, ok mun þar koma frá þér bæði mikill ætt ok góð, ok yfir þínum kynkvíslum skína bjartari geislar]

The Icelandic bishops and King James would have been pleased to hear that they had such a distinguished ancestry.

The historical works of the period, of which three are particularly important for the purposes of this book, are in some ways similar to the sagas. The *Book of Icelanders* (*Íslendingabók*) is an account by Ari Thorgilsson of the principal Norse families who settled Iceland in the late ninth and tenth centuries, and of their successors up to 1118. Ari's account was commissioned by the two bishops in Iceland, Ketil Thosteinsson of Hólar, and one of the bishops who features in the sagas, Thorlak Runolfsson of Skálholt. Ari's purpose was to reconstruct the institutional history of the young nation, especially the Althing (see Glossary) and the church, and, of necessity, he drew on oral sources. When Ari was a young man, his elderly uncle Thorkell Gellison told him that when he had visited Greenland, he had spoken to an unnamed settler who had followed Eirik to Greenland, who gave an account of the early days of the settlement. The gap between the founding of the settlement c. 985 and the compilation of Ari's account c. 1130 is c.145 years, a period short enough for elements of truth to survive and long enough for legends to intrude.

Similarly, the *Book of Settlements* (*Landnámabók*), an account of the settlement period by several authors, draws on oral sources. It exists in five versions (one only a fragment), three of which are medieval and two from the seventeenth century. The earliest of the five, known as *Sturlubók*, was originally written in the late 1270s. The manuscript was lost in the fire of Copenhagen in 1728, but survives in a copy made in 1651 by an Icelandic priest called Jón Erlendsson of Villingaholt, whose transcriptions of sagas for the Bishop of Skáholt are a valuable resource. These five versions derive from two lost early versions. At the time that these lost early versions were written, six or seven generations of settlers had been living in Iceland, and it was their family traditions that were the most important source of information. Like the *Book of Icelanders*, the gap between settlement and writing creates a measure of uncertainly about the accuracy of the accounts.

The third important work is Adam of Bremen's 'Description of the Northern Islands' (*Descriptio insularum aquilonis*), which is the fourth part of a late eleventh-century Latin treatise on the 'Deeds of the Bishops of Hamburg' (*Gesta Hammaburgensis ecclesiae pontificum*), which seems to have been commissioned by Archbishop Adalbert of Hamburg, who was also Bishop of Bremen. Adam gleaned material on Scandinavia during a period at the court of Sweyn II Estridsson of Denmark, and again his sources were oral.

In short, the sagas constitute a distinguished literary version of the oral history that is embedded in the historical works. Neither genre is history as it is now written. Together the sagas and histories constitute a corpus of founding myths, focussed either on family traditions or episcopal traditions. Such history is not hagiography, in that it can be critical, but nonetheless has an underlying purpose to glorify the family or the episcopate, not simply to illuminate the past. They may well embody fragments of truth, but the fragments are hard to identify. The *Book of Settlements* and the two Vinland Sagas give broadly similar accounts of Norse expansion to the west, but they are not independent witnesses. We need not subscribe to the view of the Bellman in Lewis Carroll's 'Hunting of the Snark' that 'what I tell you three times is true'.

The sources share a similar cast of characters, but differ in many details. Their common ground is a narrative that has the Norse settling Greenland c. 985 and, within a few years, visiting the lands to the west. In the *Saga of the Greenlanders*, the first person to see the wooded coast of these lands is an Icelandic merchant captain called Bjarni Herjolfsson, who worked principally in Norway, but spent the winters with his parents in Iceland. In 986 he returned to Iceland, only to discover that his parents had emigrated to Greenland with Eirik the Red. Bjarni decided to join his parents, but was blown off course by bad weather and driven past the southern tip of Greenland. When the weather cleared, he could see a wooded coast with low hills. He did not land, but instead sailed north, eventually reaching a barren land with substantial mountains. Neither of these places corresponded to his sense of the appearance of Greenland, but as he was on the right latitude for his parents' home at Herjolfsnes, he turned east and sailed directly to his parents' farm. Bjarni had visited this coast accidentally, and his purpose was to reach Greenland rather than explore.

The exploration, according to the *Saga of the Greenlanders*, was undertaken by Leif Eirikson, who bought Bjarni's ship and retraced his course in reverse. He came first to a stony country that he called Helluland, then sailed south to the wooded coast that he called Markland. Finally, he sailed to the south-west and landed in a more temperate place, where he spent the winter. The fishing was good, and the moderate climate and good pasture meant that his cattle were able to forage throughout the winter. Tyrkir, Leif's German slave, discovered wild grapes growing on trees, and Leif named the territory Vinland. Leif ordered the harvesting of both grapes and trees, and returned to Greenland, stopping to rescue sailors who had been shipwrecked.

Leif never returned to Vinland, but other four more voyages followed. First, Leif's half-brother Thorvald attempted to sail to Vinland. On encountering eight skrælings (see Glossary) sleeping under their skin boats, Thorvald's men managed to kill seven of them; the next day Thorvald was killed with an arrow, and the survivors returned home to Greenland. Second, Leif's full brother, Thorstein, sailed towards Vinland in an attempt to recover Thorvald's body. They were blown off course and spent the summer in storms that took them back and forth on the Atlantic. They eventually returned home, and the next winter Thorstein died. His widow Gudrid later married a visiting Icelandic trader, Thorfinn Karlsefni. Third, Gudrid persuaded Thorfinn to mount an expedition to Vinland, of which she was a member. They travelled to Vinland, and established a camp at Leifsbudir. Gudrid gave birth to a son, Snorri, and the Norse traded milk for furs with the skrælings. The following spring the skrælings attacked, and the colony was abandoned. Fourth, Freydis (Eirik the Red's daughter) and her husband Thorvard established a partnership with two Icelandic traders, the brothers Finnbogi and Helgi. They arrived at Leifsbudir, where Freydis and her husband occupied Leif's accommodation, and the Icelanders established a camp further inland. Freydis deceptively persuaded her husband and his crew to kill the Icelanders and their crew (including the women), and then returned to Greenland with the cargo, explaining that the Icelanders had remained in Leifsbudir.

The *Saga of Eirik the Red* has a different version of events. Leif is said to have travelled to Norway, where he spent the winter as an attendant at the court of King Olaf Tryggvesson, who was instrumental in the conversion of Norway to Christianity. Leif was baptized in the Christian faith and set sail to Greenland with a priest with a view to converting the Norse Greenlanders to Christianity. He was blown off course, arrived at an unknown shore to the west of Greenland, where he found wild grapes, self-sown wheat, and trees called *mösurr* (possibly maples); he called it Vinland. After loading his ship, he sailed to Greenland (again), en route stopping to rescue shipwrecked sailors. Leif's mother Thjodhild converted to Christianity and built a small church at Brattahlid, but his father Eirik declined to convert, whereupon Thjodhild committed herself to celibacy.

The following year, Leif's half-brother Thorstein made an unsuccessful voyage to the land that Leif had found, but was caught by storms and blown east as far as Ireland. He returned home and married Gudrid, but soon died. Gudrid subsequently married Thorfinn Karlsefni, and they decided to establish a colony in Vinland together with Thorfinn's Icelandic partners, Bjarni and Thorhall. Thorfinn's expedition, consisting of some 160 men and women (including Eirik the Red's son Thorvald), embarked from the Eastern Settlement, sailed north-west to the Western Settlement, to then turned west to sail to Helluland. They sailed south, and eventually arrived at a promising bay, whereupon Thorfinn despatched two fleet-footed Scottish slaves, Haki and Hekla, to run inland, returning within three days. The Scots returned carrying self-sown wheat and wild grapes, and reported good pasturage. This episode, as reported in the saga, has clearly become dislocated, as it should be set in Hop, which was further south. The expedition continued southwards, camped on an island that they named Straumey, and endured a difficult winter. Ten of the prospective settlers, led by Thorhall the Hunter, decided to try to find Vinland in the north, but were blown off course to Ireland, where they were enslaved. The others continued south with Thorfinn in search of Vinland. They landed at a site that they called Hop, which means 'tidal lagoon', setting up camp on the shore of a river at a point at which it had widened into a lake. They found self-sown wheat and 'grape-trees' (*vínviðr*), which may have been grape vines growing on trees.

After a hostile encounter with skrælings, the Norse retreated, pausing as they left to murder five sleeping skrælings. The colony was abandoned, and Thorfinn sailed north to search for Thorhall the Hunter and his men. At one of their landings, Eirik's son Thorvald was killed by an arrow shot by a uniped (*einfœtingr*). The expedition then returned to Greenland, stopping en route in Markland to capture two skræling children, whom they baptized and taught to speak Norse. The boys are unnamed, but their mother is said to be Vætilld, their father Uvægi, and their kings Avalldamon and Avalldida. Linguists have not been to associate the names with either Innu-aimun (the Algonquian language of the Innu) or Nunatsiavut (the Inuktitut dialect spoken in Labrador); the language of the Dorset is unknown. These are the only aboriginal names recorded in Norse sources, but it is unclear whether these unfortunate captive skrælings were Innu, Inuit, or Dorset.

How much of the sagas is true? It is clear from the archaeology of the Eastern Arctic and the L'Anse aux Meadows site that voyages to the west did take place. It is also likely that southern Labrador was visited, principally to harvest wood, as Greenland's dwarf trees were not sufficient for the needs of the Greenland Norse for shipbuilding, even when supplemented by driftwood. The identification of Labrador south of the treeline with Markland is encouraged by sources outside the sagas. The last known reference to Markland occurs in the Skálholt annals (*Skálholtsannáll*), which has an entry for 1347 in which a small ship from Greenland, shorn of its anchor, 'had travelled to Markland and then was driven here by a storm' (*höfðu farit til Marklandz enn siðan vordit hingat hafreka*). The laconic tone of the entry implies a routine trip, perhaps to harvest timber in Markland. The settlement at Hop may have existed. In 2018 Birgitta Wallace, the respected archaeologist associated with L'Anse aux Meadows, announced her conviction that Hop was a settlement (or a group of seasonal settlements) in the Miramichi and Chaleur Bay area of north-eastern New Brunswick, which is the only place that matches all the details in in the sagas: it has barrier sandbars, produces wild grapes and salmon, and has indigenous people (the Mi'kmaq) that used canoes made with animal hide.

The sagas and related historical works propose a geography that is in significant part imagined, but is sometimes anchored in the real world that travellers had visited. The people whose stories are told in sagas and histories hover in the awkward space between fact and fiction, and it is difficult to place them on the continuum that connects the end points. One example is the claim, in several of the Icelandic annals (like the sagas, derived from oral sources), that in 1121 Bishop Eirik from Greenland went in search of Vinland (*Eirikr byskup af Grœnlandi leitaði Vinlands*). This is Eirik Gnupsson, whose diocese would have included a Norse Greenlandic colony in Vinland as well as Greenland.

Bishop Eirik is at best an obscure figure, and in the absence of hard evidence, some have used their imaginations to fill the void. In 1872 Richard Clarke published the first volume (of three) of his scholarly *Lives of deceased bishops of the Catholic Church of the United States*. The lives are arranged chronologically, and the first bishop of the United States is said to have been Eirik Gnupsson. Clarke declares that 'westward was the triumphant march of the cross', and that a divine hand guided 'the agencies for a future and distant advance of Christianity from the Eastern to the Western hemisphere...destined to restore to the Church in America much of what it had lost in Europe.' Clarke describes Bishop Eirik's visit to the Church of Vinland, in the Norse colony on the shores of Narragansett Bay, near Newport, Rhode Island, where the church that he erected still stands (see chapter 8; Fig. 8.3). Bishop Eirik realized that the infant Church of Vinland needed him more than the well-established church in Greenland, and so, 'laying aside the mitre and crosier, he assumed that black cassock and the cross of the humble missionary, and resigned his bishopric'. After years of service to both the Norse colonists and the local Native Americans, Eirik died a martyr, and so America's 'first of bishops' became its 'first of martyrs'. The chapter concludes with a call for 'the title Bishop of Gardar [to] be revived in our venerable hierarchy, and bestowed upon one of the Vicars Apostolic or Bishops *in partibus infidelium* ['in the lands of the unbelievers']'. This vision was to be realized in 1996, when the titular bishopric of Gardar was nominally restored; the first incumbent, appointed in 2001, is Edward Clark, auxiliary bishop of Los Angeles. Thus is untrammelled fantasy transformed into public history.

Within the sagas, the characters seem distinctly literary: pagan Eirik is contrasted with Christian Leif, virtuous Gudrid with wicked Freydis. The existence of such characters has not been attested in the archaeological record. Such corroboration is of course possible. In 1961, an excavation in Israel yielded a piece of limestone inscribed with the words '[PONTI]US PILATUS/ [PRAEF]ECTUS IUDA[EA]E' ('Pontius Pilate, prefect of Judea'), thus confirming the historicity of a character otherwise known only from literary sources, including the New Testament. Indeed, more than fifty characters in the Hebrew Bible have been attested in the archaeological record. In the Norse world, runic inscriptions often mention personal names. Some 160 runic inscriptions have been found in Norse Greenland, but no personal names from the sagas have been found. The discovery of a Norse version of the Pilate Stone would change everything, but until such a discovery is made, it would be unwise to affirm unequivocally the historicity of any figure in the sagas.

Of the places that Leif is said in the sagas to have visited, the one that attracts most interest is Vinland, because of the possibility that it was located in what is now the United States. Those determined to use the sagas as logbooks have seized on the line in the *Saga of the Greenlanders* that declares,

> Day and night were of more equal duration than in Greenland or Iceland. On the shortest day of the year the sun was up by 9.00 a.m. and did not set until after 3.00 p.m.

> [*Meira var þar jafn-dægri en á Grænlandi eða Íslandi. Sól hafði þar eyktar-stað ok dagmála-stað um skammdegi*]

My translation obscures several difficulties. *Jafn-dægri* is the winter equinox, so relatively straightforward, but *dagmála-staðr* means (roughly) the place of the sun at breakfast-time, i.e. between 8.00 a.m. and 9.00 a.m., and is used as the equivalent of *terce* in the liturgical hours, and so means 9.00 a.m., Similarly, *eyktar-staðr* (the subject of much academic discussion) denotes the position of the sun at 3.30 p.m., though it is often used as the equivalent of *none* in the liturgical hours, and so means 3.00 p.m. These terms were not precise, and difficult to determine in practice, because the astronomical calculations are complex. There was also no way of calculating longitude. As a result, Vinland has been located as far north as 58° 26' (the latitude of Juneau, Alaska, and Ungava Bay, where not many grapes are grown) and as far south as 31° N, which is the border between Alabama and Florida (and in the late eighteenth century was the border between the United States and Spanish Florida). In terms of longitude, it has also been proposed that Vinland was in the Great Lakes area. In short, the information in the saga can place Vinland wherever one wants it to be.

The sagas were not alone in describing places called Helluland, Markland, and Vinland. The lands to the west of Greenland began to be named by Europeans in the eleventh century. In the mid eleventh century, the German chronicler Adam of Bremen

visited the court (in Roskilde) of the Danish King Sweyn II
Estridsson, who

> spoke of an island which is called Vinland, because the grapes that
> grow wild there yield wine of the highest quality. Moreover, the
> assertion that self-seeded grain grows there in abundance is not
> fanciful, but, as we know from the reliable accounts of the Danes,
> true.

> [*Praeterea umam adhuc insulam recitavit a multis in eo repertam occeano,
> quae dicitur Winland, eo quod ibi vites sponte nascantur, vinum optimum
> ferentes. Nam et fruges ibi non seminatas habundare, non fabulosa opinione,
> sed certa comperimus relatione Danorum*]

Adam insists that his report is not fanciful (*non fabulosa opinione*).
He is correct, in the sense that it was based on accounts that he
had heard from apparently reliable sources, notably that of the
king of Denmark.

All three western lands are mentioned in a thirteenth-century
geographical treatise known as *Landafræði* ('land knowledge'):

> South from Greenland there is Helluland, then Markland; from
> there it is not a great distance to Vinland the Good, which some
> men think extends from Africa, and, if that is the case, then the
> inland sea must lie between Vinland and Markland

> [*Sudr frá Grenlandi er Helluland, þa er Markland, þa er eigi langt til
> Vinlandz ens goda, er sumir menn ætla at gangi af Affrika, ok ef sva er, þa er
> úthaf innfallanda a milli Vinlandz ok Marklandz*]

Another variation on this uncertain positioning of Vinland may
be found in a fragmentary encyclopaedic work (possibly from
the fifteenth century) called *Gripla* ('little compendium'), which
explains that beyond Greenland

> there lies a land called Furdustrands, which heavy frosts render
> uninhabitable, as far as anyone knows. South from there is

Helluland, which is called the land of the Skrælings. From there it is not a great distance to Vinland the Good, which some men think extends from Africa. Between Vinland and Greenland is Ginnungagap.

[*Furðustrandir heitir land; þar eru frost mikil, so ekki er byggjanda so menn viti. Suður frá er Helluland, þat er kallað Skrælingjaland. Þá er skammt til Vinlands hin[s] góða, er sumir menn ætla að gangi af Affrika. Milli Vinland og Grænlands er Ginnungagap*]

In the cosmology of Norse mythology, Ginnungagap is the primordial void, another imagined space. It was, however, sufficiently substantial to appear on maps of the region drawn several centuries later. It is to those maps that we must now turn.

CHAPTER 3

MAPS

The Norse did not make maps, but others made maps that depicted territories reached by the Norse as they expanded westwards into the North Atlantic. The cartography of these maps is based on the charting of coastlines when Western Europe is depicted, but in the North Atlantic it is shaped by written sources, ideology, and, on occasion, fraudulent intention.

The Anglo-Saxon Mappa Mundi (held by the British Library) was probably the work of a scribe based in Canterbury in the second quarter of the eleventh century. The map depicts the provinces of the Roman Empire, including Britannia. The level of detail in the depiction of the Atlantic archipelago is unprecedented. Britain and Ireland are readily recognisable, but so are smaller islands, including the Isle of Man, the Isle of Wight, the Scillies, and the Channel Islands. The islands to the north extend beyond Orkney and Shetland to the Faeroes and Iceland, which were known to Irish monks and Norse seafarers.

Greenland is first shown in a map of 1427, recently established to be the work of the Danish cleric known variously as Claudius Clavus and Nicholaus Niger. This map, which is held by the Bibliothèque Publique in Nancy, depicts the east coast of Greenland as a peninsula descending from a northern land mass (populated by unipeds) that extends eastward to the sea above

Scandinavia (where it is inhabited by pygmies). Greenland is labelled *Gronlandia provincia* (in the sense of an ecclesiastical province), and a faint mark, used elsewhere on the map to indicate population centres, indicates the location of Gardar, the episcopal seat. The difficulty is that the Norse settlements, including Gardar, were on the west coast, not the largely inaccessible east coast. Claudius Clavus had depended on written Latin sources such as Adam of Bremen and Saxo Grammaticus (he had no access to the sagas), and had unwisely (but understandably) assumed that Gardar would be somewhere on the east coast.

Later maps have an important political dimension. The voyages of Bartholomeu Dias (who rounded the Cape of Good Hope in 1488) and Columbus gave rise to rival Portuguese claims by Portugal and Spain with respect to sovereignty over lands in Asia and America. The kings of Spain and Portugal applied to Pope Alexander VI to divide the world in half for the purposes of exploration and exploitation. In 1493 the Pope obliged by issuing a bull that drew the dividing line from pole to pole 100 leagues west of the Azores and the Cape Verde Islands: Portugal was to have the right of exploration and conquest in lands to the east, and Spain would have the same right in lands to the west. The Portuguese protested, and the two sides met in Tordesillas, Spain, to settle the dispute. On 7 June 1494 the treaty was signed, shifting the line 270 leagues further west, to approximately the 50th degree of longitude west of Greenwich, which strikes the mainland of South America close to the mouth of the Amazon. This new arrangement allowed Portugal to claim Brazil on 22 April 1500.

Establishing longitude was an inexact science, and few people had first-hand experience of regions remote from Europe. Such factors enabled cartographers to draft maps that accommodated political considerations. One such map, now in the Bibliothèque Nationale in Paris, was drawn c. 1503 by the Genoese cartographer Nicolò Caveri (traditionally known as Nicolò Canerio, due to a misreading of the map). The Caveri map incorporated Portuguese cartography. Greenland is included, as is an island that represents Newfoundland and Labrador. This composite island has been shifted to the east to bring it to the Portuguese side of the Tordesillas line, and so both this island and Greenland are marked with Portuguese flags.

In 1558 a prominent Venetian called Nicolò Zen (in standard Italian, 'Niccolò Zeno') published a map of the North Atlantic purporting to illustrate the travels in the 1380s of two of his ancestors, the brothers Nicolò and Antonio Zen. This map, together with a collection of letters, demonstrated that America had not been discovered by a Genoese, but by Venetian patricians. Greenland is shown, as is the tip of Estotilandia, which clearly represents Labrador. There is also a phantom island called Frisland, and such was the credibility of the map, Frisland continued to appear on maps for a century. That credibility was unwarranted: the Zen Map has the dubious honour of being the earliest faked evidence of a European presence in the Americas. The map has been copied from a variety of earlier maps, and the letters describing the lost Norse colony in Greenland and the discovery of America are forgeries. There are a few Venetians who still maintain that the letters are authentic. There is little point in challenging their conviction.

Three maps of Scandinavian origin, all now in the Royal Library (Det Kongelige Bibliotek) in Copenhagen, might be thought to be too late to yield useful information about the Norse, but they certainly reveal attitudes to Norse expeditions in the North

Fig. 3.1 Skálholt Map, Royal Library, Copenhagen

Atlantic. The best known of the three is the Skálholt Map (also known as the Stefánsson Map) (Fig. 3.1). Medieval Iceland was divided into two dioceses, and the episcopal seats were at Hólar (in the north) and Skálholt (in the south). Both are now attractive villages that evoke their past in a few fine historic buildings that remain. The first version of the Skálholt Map was drawn in 1590 (later copied incorrectly as 1570) by Sigurd Stefánsson, the head of the cathedral school in Skálholt. Sigurd's original is lost, but a copy made in 1669 by Thórdur Thorlaksson (the future Lutheran bishop of Skálholt) survives. This map draws on contemporary cartographic knowledge, the inheritance of the Zen brothers, and the stories in the Vinland Sagas and Icelandic annals.

The Skálholt Map shows the islands of Britannia, Irland (Ireland), Orcades (Orkney), Hetland (Shetland), Feroe (Faroes), Island (Iceland), and the phantom islands of Frisland and Narve Oe (possibly the 'Island of Narfi', a character in Norse mythology). It also depicts Greenland (Gronlandia), which is shown as a peninsula. The Norse colony on Greenland had long disappeared, but the two place names on the map of Greenland are significant. On the north-east coast, a glaciated mountain called Hvitserkr (literally 'white shirt') is marked; this was the landmark for which Icelandic seafarers scanned the horizon when sailing west from the Snæfell Peninsula. The other place name is Herjolfsnes, the Norse settlement (near Cape Farewell) that features in the Vinland Sagas; the late date of some of the clothing excavated in its graveyard may imply that Herjolfsnes was one of the last surviving homesteads in the Eastern Settlement. Areas on the mainland are marked as Helleland, Markland, Skrælinge Land, and Promontorium Winlandiæ (Vinland Promontory).

The place names Helluland (as it is spelt in the sagas) and Markland clearly derive from literary sources. A marginal note (in Latin) in the handwriting of Bishop Thórdur (presumably copying Sigurd's annotations), keyed to the map by the letter A, explains that Skrælinge Land was the habitation of people encountered by the English, which must refer to Martin Frobisher and John Davis. A note keyed to B explains that Vinland, called Vinland the Good because of its fertility, has previously been thought by 'our countrymen' to end in the Southern Ocean, but that recent accounts show it to be separated from the American mainland only by a fjord or a sound. The presence of Vinland on the map has long attracted interest by those eager to show that the Norse reached America before Columbus. The resemblance of the peninsula to the northern peninsula of Newfoundland was one of the factors that led to exploration of the peninsula and the discovery of genuine Norse ruins at L'Anse aux Meadows. And in a circular argument, the discovery of the site at L'Anse aux Meadows has been deemed to show that the Skálholt Map is based not simply on contemporary cartography and literary sources, but also on knowledge of the Norse discovery of America, which had by unknown means been transmitted down the centuries to the map of Sigurd Stefánsson.

The second map was drawn in 1605 by Hans Poulsen Resen, a Copenhagen professor who was later consecrated as a bishop. The Resen Map was drawn in the wake of a Danish expedition to Greenland in search of the Norse colonies. Like the Skálholt Map (which was either a source, or the common descendant of an unknown source), the Resen Map represents Vinland as a thin peninsula extending to the north from a land mass called Norumbega, a place name that was to recur in various locations in North America.

The third map was drawn in 1606 by Gudbrandur Thorlaksson, bishop of Hólar (and an accomplished mathematician and cartographer). The map is endorsed by Resen as being in the hand of Bishop Gudbrandur. This is a plausible attribution: Bishop Gudbrandur was a better cartographer than his predecessors, and his map was also informed by recent accounts of voyages to Greenland. The principal advance of this map over its predecessors is the orientation of Greenland, which is still a peninsula, but extends south-west rather than south-east. The southern extremity of Greenland is portrayed as a coast with two deep fjords. The eastern fjord is identified as Eiriksfjord, and the unnamed western fjord is said to be the site of the Western Settlement. A further note explains that to the south of this coast, across a body of water (identified as the Ginnungagap, the primordial void of Norse mythology), lies America, where 'our forefathers' voyaged when they found Vinland.

All three maps were drawn by men who had never been further west than Iceland, so they reflect perceptions rather than the results of surveying, but it is their purpose that commands interest. Sigurd Stefánsson, Thórdur Thorlaksson, Hans Poulsen Resen, and Gudbrandur Thorlaksson were all Lutherans, and their maps stake a Protestant claim to the discovery of the New World prior to the voyages of Columbus.

The implications of such maps have long been the subject of occasional scholarly assessment, but only rose to prominence with the discovery of the Vinland map (Fig. 3.2).

On 11 October 1965, the day before America's Columbus Day, Yale University Library announced that it had acquired a hand-drawn map of the known world (Latin: *mappa mundi*) dating from c. 1440. The map included a depiction of the coast of North America that the Norse had discovered and named Vinland, and declared in a note that Vinland had been 'discovered by Bjarni and Leif'. Here at last was proof of the Norse discovery of America prior to Columbus. The Associated Press account was typical:

> Yale University scholars sliced the frosting off Christopher Columbus' birthday cake Sunday. They've found an ancient map which they say proves that Leif Ericson and other Vikings had

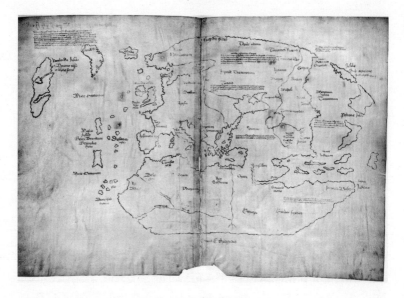

Fig. 3.2 Vinland Map

explored North America long before Columbus set sail. The map was drawn about 1440 A.D., half a century before Columbus' voyage—probably by a monk in Basel, Switzerland, using source materials dating back at least to the 13th century, the Yale University Library announced. Greenland is drawn very accurately on the parchment map, and to the west is "Vinland."

The next day, Yale University Press published a substantial account of the map called *The Vinland Map and the Tartar Relation*. The book had been prepared in secret by three eminent scholars, two British and one American. The lead author was Raleigh Skelton, superintendent of the Map Room at the British Museum. Skelton had been trained as a modern linguist (French and German) at Cambridge and had earned a reputation as a distinguished authority on historical cartography, particularly on the maps of the Age of Exploration. The second author was Thomas E. Marston, a former collector who had become curator of medieval and Renaissance manuscripts at Yale's Beinecke Library, where the map was kept. The third author was George Painter, deputy curator of incunabula at the British Museum. Painter had studied classics at Cambridge and was a student of modern French literature; his two-volume biography of Proust still commands respect. All three were honourable scholars, and to disagree with their judgements is not to impugn their integrity.

Scholars want to be confident about their conclusions before they publish, and so often consult colleagues with specialist expertise while conducting their research. The three authors of the Yale volume were bound to secrecy and so could not consult colleagues working in areas in which they lacked expertise. None of the authors had expertise in Scandinavian languages or history, but they could not consult Scandinavian specialists; similarly, none had a close knowledge of fifteenth-century Gothic cursive script, but they could not consult handwriting experts. These were strictures that would eventually be seen to have come with a grievous cost.

The map that was revealed to the world had a complex context. It was bound with a short manuscript treatise called *Hystoria Tartarorum*, which the editors translated as the *Tartar Relation*; the author was identified as 'Friar C. de Bridia'—the initial is not expanded into a name, nor can the place name 'Bridia' be confidently identified. This was a hitherto unknown account of a well-known expedition of the Franciscan papal legate Giovanni da Pian del Carpine across Asia to the court of the Mongols in 1245–47. The map and the treatise had evidently been bound together for some time, but the wormholes did not quite match. Investigation soon brought a second manuscript into play. In 1958

Thomas Marston had acquired for Yale a tattered medieval copy of books 21–24 of the *Speculum historiale* (The Mirror of History) assembled by the Dominican encyclopaedist Vincent of Beauvais, and when the three documents were put together (map, *Speculum*, *Hystoria*), the wormholes aligned perfectly. The wormholes, endearingly described by George Painter as 'the dear little worms' serrated tooth marks', confirmed to the investigators that the Vinland Map was genuine. Handwriting in all three manuscripts was observed to be identical. The paper in the mixed parchment and paper quires of the text manuscripts was observed to have identical watermarks of a known fifteenth-century type.

When the book was released and the map put on display, there was rejoicing that the Norse discovery of America was now a settled fact. Some academic reviewers, however, were puzzled by several features of the map (Fig. 3.3). The remarkably accurate map of Greenland, for example, depicts it as an island, whereas previous maps had shown it as a peninsula. Northern Greenland is not known to have been surveyed until the early twentieth century, so the outline of the northern coast is remarkably perspicacious. Others raised doubts about the cartography, and still others about the handwriting. In view of such doubts, the Smithsonian Institution in Washington, DC, decided to convene a conference to discuss the issues raised by reviewers. The reservations aired at that conference continue to resonate half a century later, and to inform academic and popular debate about the authenticity of the map.

Academic arguments about the map initially focussed on the legends, the cartography, the physical properties of the manuscript, and the question of provenance. Two of the legends, both in the upper left section of the map, are of particular interest.

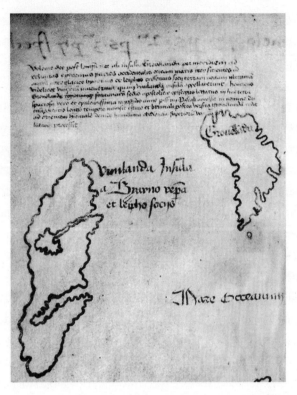

Fig. 3.3 Vinland Map detail showing Vinland and Greenland

The legend to the upper right of the island of Vinland reads *Vinlanda Insula a Byarno rep[art]a et leipho sociis* (the island of Vinland, discovered by Bjarni and Leif together). Leif is clearly Leif Eirikson, but who is the Bjarni who accompanied him? There are two characters named Bjarni in the Vinland Sagas. Bjarni Herjólfsson was the first to sight Helluland and Markland. Leif subsequently bought this Bjarni's ship, retraced his voyage, and discovered Vinland. They did not sail together. The only other Bjarni was Bjarni Grímolfsson, an Icelandic shipowner associated with Eirik the Red and Thorfinn Karlsefni. Like his namesake, this Bjarni is never said to have gone to Vinland. Raleigh Skelton argued that the author of the legend either misremembered the sagas, or was drawing on an otherwise unknown source for the contention that someone called Bjarni accompanied Leif.

There is, however, another possible explanation for the contention that Bjarni and Leif sailed together to Vinland. The historian Kirsten Seaver discovered that the error was introduced in a *Historie von Grönland* published in 1765 by David Crantz, who had spent a year in Greenland as a missionary for the Moravian Church. Crantz's treatise was soon translated into French and English, and so his error was replicated and perpetuated. This discovery may imply that the Vinland Map was prepared after 1765 by someone who had read Crantz.

The longer legend in the upper-left corner repeats the claim that Leif and Bjarni together discovered Vinland. The Old Norse specialist Peter Foote, who had an excellent command of late medieval Latin, noted that in this legend Leif Eirikson is named as *leiphus erissonius* by someone who did not realise that Eirikson is a patronymic, not a surname. A Scandinavian writer would have Latinized 'Leifr Eiríksson' as *Erici* or *Erici filius*. Foote's other examples include the map's repeated rendering of the Norse suffix '-land' as 'landa' (Vinlanda, Isolanda, Ierlanda), whereas a medieval Scandinavian would have used a 'landia' suffix. The sagas were unknown outside of Scandinavia, so the author must have come from that region, but his ignorance of naming conventions suggests otherwise.

The parchment of the map is in poor condition compared to that of the two text manuscripts, and is pale by comparison. Analysis has shown that at some point the map parchment has been rigorously cleaned, perhaps to remove earlier written or drawn material on the surface, and its pallor is a consequence of scrubbing. Even the wormhole linings are pallid compared to those in the other texts, which have an orange hue and fluoresce under ultraviolet light. It was argued that a forger introduced live 'bookworms' (one of several insects capable of boring through books) into the manuscripts, as previous forgers have done, but it was also observed that the parchment on which the map was later to be drawn was in the assembled manuscripts at an earlier stage.

The handwriting of the legends is also problematical. The claim that the same hand wrote the legends on the map and the two treatises has been repeatedly challenged by specialists. One particularly troubling feature of the Latin legends on the map is the occasional use of the ligature 'æ', which in classical Latin represented a distinct diphthong. In the medieval period the 'æ' gradually disappeared, only to be revived in the classicizing humanist script championed by fifteenth-century Italian humanists. There is no known instance, except on the legends of the Vinland Map, of the ligature being used in the cursive Gothic script in which the legends are written. The fact that 'æ' is sometimes written as 'ae' (as in the legend beside two Atlantic islands that concludes *Branziliæ Dictae*) is also troubling.

Cartographical issues include an island called Desiderate, situated in the approximate region of the Azores. The term is not used on any other medieval map. However, the island that Columbus named Deseada (Spanish, 'the desired one'), which is now La Désirade (part of the French overseas *département* of Guadeloupe) began to appear on maps in 1500. A similar issue arises with respect to the depiction of what appears to be the Japanese archipelago. As Skelton acknowledges, the islands include not only Honshu, but Hokkaido and the Russian island of

Sakhalin, which are unknown in any other fifteenth-century maps. Sakhalin, for example, is not known to have been seen by a European prior to a Dutch visit of 1643. Such apparent anachronisms are troubling.

Provenance also proved to be a perplexing issue. The volume containing the Vinland Map and the *Tartar Relation* first appeared in 1957, when Enzo Ferrajoli de Ry, an Italian book dealer living in Spain, began to show it to booksellers in Geneva and Paris, and possibly to others in Italy and Spain. Eventually the volume was brought to England, where a London book dealer called Irving Davis, possibly accompanied by Ferrajoli, offered it to the British Museum, either for a scholarly judgement or as a possible purchase. Accounts of who brought it to the museum and of which museum staff inspected it vary, but it seems clear that those who saw it included Raleigh Skelton and George Painter, who were to become two of the principals in the Yale volume. It was also seen by Bertram Schofield, the keeper of manuscripts, and it was he who rejected the map, partly because it lacked provenance, and partly because his trained palaeographer's eye had detected modern features in the handwriting of the legends.

Ferrajoli then sold the book for $3,500 to an American dealer called Laurence C. Witten II, who in subsequent years gave widely varying accounts of what he knew about the provenance of the manuscript. Witten was a Yale graduate, and offered it to the Yale's Beinecke Library, which hesitated because of the discrepant wormholes. Within months, however, Thomas Marston, curator of medieval and Renaissance manuscripts at the Beinecke Library (and a friend of Witten), had bought the *Speculum historiale* manuscript from Irving Davis, Ferrajoli's London associate. Witten said that the Vinland volume had come from a private library, but was not willing to reveal the owner's name, as the owner wished to keep his affairs from the tax authorities. The only sign of previous ownership was an erased stamp in the *Speculum* manuscript. Stamps of private ownership are generally to be found in front matter, but public libraries either consistently use a fixed page (often page 51 or 101) or a random page. An erased stamp in an interior page therefore hints at public rather than private ownership.

At this point Yale approached Paul Mellon, a Yale alumnus and donor, to ask if he would buy the manuscript and donate it to the Beinecke. Mellon agreed to pay a negotiated price of c. $300,000, on condition that it could be proven to be authentic. He insisted that both his name and the existence of the map be kept secret until a scholarly assessment of its authenticity had been published. By 1964 *The Vinland Map and the Tartar Relation* was in proof, and Mellon bought and donated the manuscript to Yale, requesting that the gift be anonymous.

The publication of the book and the exhibition of the map were not received as warmly as Yale had hoped. Unease among academics was widespread, and so in 1966 the historian Wilcomb Washburn organized a conference at the Smithsonian Institution in Washington, DC. The conference fuelled doubts about the authenticity of the map, and Witten's credibility as a witness began to fray. He implied that he had visited the private library where the manuscript had been kept and had been assured by the owner that, although he did not know the origin of the manuscript, it had been in his family for several generations. Witten was later to admit that he had neither visited the library nor spoken to the owner. Witten also chose to defend the reputation of Enzo Ferrajoli, who in 1961 he had been imprisoned for eighteen months for stealing books from the library of Zaragoza Cathedral (Biblioteca Capitular de la Seo). Witten insisted that Ferrajoli was innocent, and that the cathedral had sold the books to him.

In 1974 the ink on the Vinland Map was analysed by Walter and Lucy McCrone, who were prominent research chemists in Chicago. The McCrones lifted twenty-nine ink particles from the map, and discovered that the ink contained significant quantities of anatase, a pigment derived from titanium oxide that had only been available since the 1920s. In the wake of this announcement, Yale University Library acknowledged that 'the famous Vinland Map may be a forgery'. Helen Wallis (map librarian at the British Library) organized a symposium at the Royal Geographical Society in London. The McCrones attended and presented a detailed account of their research; their findings were widely reported in the European and American press. Their discovery that the ink was made in the twentieth century should have ended the argument in favour of the map being a forgery, but vested interests, including those of Yale University Press and many amateur enthusiasts determined to prove that the Vikings had preceded Columbus, meant that the debate lived on.

In 1995 Yale University Press mounted a final defence against the tide of science, publishing a revised and updated edition of its 1965 volume, intended, in the words of its publisher, 'to lead to the rehabilitation of one of history's most important cartographic finds'. George Painter, the only survivor of the three original authors, wrote a defiant introduction to the new edition, adducing evidence that the McCrones' analysis was flawed. In a ringing peroration, Painter concludes that,

> the Vinland Map now reappears as a major and authentic message
> from the middle ages, on a hitherto unknown moment in the

history of the world and American discovery. It is a true voice from
the past, which still lives and need never be silent again.

The academic community was not convinced.

Investigation of the map continued, as it has up to the present.
In 2004 Kirsten Seaver published a formidable book-length study
called *Myths, and Men: The Story of the Vinland Map*. Seaver's assiduous
research into the historical issues, her multidisciplinary approach,
and her knowledge of Scandinavian languages and culture, enabled
her to deal the death blow to claims that the map is authentic. She
also proposed a possible forger, Father Josef Fischer, an Austrian
Jesuit with expertise in cartography.

In 2013 John Paul Floyd, an independent Scottish researcher,
announced that he had identified the provenance of both the
Speculum and *Tartar Relation* manuscripts in the catalogue of the
Exposición Histórico-Europea, an exhibition mounted in Madrid
in 1892–3 to celebrate the quatercentenary of Columbus's first voyage. Items described in the catalogue include a fifteenth-century
manuscript volume; the entry (in my translation) reads

> Vincent of Beauvais, *Speculum naturale, doctrinale, morale, historiale*.
> The present volume contains, from the celebrated encyclopaedia
> of Vincent of Beauvais, only Books 21 to 24 of the third part of
> the *Speculum historiale*. At the end has been added a treatise by the
> author Friar C. de Bridia dedicated to the Very Reverend Father
> Friar Boguslaus, minister of the Minorite friars in Bohemia
> and Poland. Manuscript, two columns, fifteenth-century script,
> the covers of each book in vellum and the rest on paper, the
> epigraphs in red ink, the place of the initials in white. It consists
> of 251 leaves.
>
> [*Vincentius bellvacensis. Speculum naturale, doctrinale, morale, historiale.
> El presente volumen contiene, de esta célebre enciclopedia de Vicente de
> Beauvais, solamente los libros 21 á 24 de la tercera parte del Speculum

historiale. Al fin se ha añadido un tratadito intitulado Historia Tartarorum
dedicado por el autor Fr. C. de Bridia, al R.P. Fr. Bogardio, ministro de los
franciscanos en Boemia y Polonia. Manuscrito, á dos columnas, letra del siglo
xv, las cubiertas de cada cuaderno en vitela y lo demás en papel, los epigrafes
en tinta roja, el lugar de las iniciales en blanco. Consta de 251 hojas].

This is clearly the volume containing the Yale manuscripts, and yet there is no mention of the map. The page count seems to confirm its absence. The catalogue explains that the volume was lent by the Archdiocese of Zaragoza. The archiepiscopal library is the library in Zaragoza Cathedral from which Enzo Ferrajoli was convicted of stealing books. Ferrajoli may have stolen the Yale volume himself, or he may have been fencing the volume on behalf of another thief. The volume was presumably stolen before 1954, when the medieval codices in the library were photographed. I do not know whether the cathedral library has asked for its manuscripts to be returned.

The catalogue's tally of 251 pages gives another hint of the state of the manuscript in 1892. The Yale *Speculum* has 239 leaves, and the *Tartar Relation* has 11 leaves with writing on them (and five blank leaves). That means that there is now one fewer leaf than existed in 1892. The missing leaf could not be the Vinland Map, which has two leaves, and so is probably the missing leaf at the beginning of Book 21 of the *Speculum*. It is reasonable to conclude that in 1892 the volume did not include the map, though it may have included the parchment on which the map was later drawn.

Floyd has capped this extraordinary discovery with a second. Cristóbal Pérez Pastor was an archivist, philologist, literary historian and bibliographer, and chaplain to the royal convent of Poor Clares (Descalzas Reales) in Madrid. Father Pérez died in 1908, and four volumes of his *Noticias y documentos relativos à la historia y literatura españolas* were published posthumously between 1910 and 1926. One entry in the third volume reads

> *Speculum historiae* (second and third part). History of the Tartars. Manuscript, fifteenth-century script, with two columns, epigraphs in red ink. Each book has the first and last pages in parchment and the rest in paper. At the end it is dated 'Completed on 30 July 1247 AD'. Folio, bound in leather with contemporary decoration. Of the *Speculum historiae* it contains books 21–24, which finish the third part of the work.
>
> [*Speculum historiae (segunda y tercera parte). Historia tartarum. Manuscrito, letra del siglo xv, a dos columnas, los epigrafes en tinta roja; cada cuaderno tiene la primera y última hojas en pergamino y las demás en papel. Al final lleva la fecha: "Actum ab incarnatione Domim M.CC.XL.VII. tertio Kalendas Augusti"; folio, encuadernado en tabla forrada de piel, con adornos de la época. Del Speculum hist contiene los libros xxj a xxiv, que dan remate a la parte tercera de la obra*].

Again, this seems to be a description of the Yale manuscript—and Father Pérez, who was a good bibliographer, does not mention the map. It would seem that the Yale volume had been in Zaragoza Cathedral for a very long time, until it was stolen in the early 1950s. Blank parchment from the volume was subsequently used to draw the Vinland Map. Father Fischer (Kirsten Seaver's candidate for the forger) died in 1944, so he cannot have been the forger.

These discoveries have emerged alongside new knowledge about the parchment on which the map is drawn. In 2017 a Danish team examined the parchment and concluded that a modern chemical (Glycerol monostearate) used as a food addictive had been applied to the surface and had soaked into the parchment. Yale has also been investigating the map seriously, for the first time since the 1980s. The university has assembled a 'Vinland Map Team' of thirteen scholars and scientists, drawing on its own formidable scientific and technical resources, supplemented by a biomolecular archaeology team at University of York (England) and two specialist laboratories. A preliminary account of their investigations was unveiled at a conference entitled 'The Vinland Map Rediscovered: New research on the forgery and its historical context' at the Mystic Seaport Museum in September 2018 (Mystic is the name of a Connecticut town, not an adjective). The chemist Richard Hark, speaking for the team, outlined a few preliminary conclusions. Inks used on *Tartar Relation* and the *Speculum historiale*, he explained, are iron gall (except for a few patches on the first page of the *Tartar Relation*), whereas the ink of the Vinland Map is a carbon-based twentieth-century ink. He went on to say that radiocarbon dating of parchment indicates that the three manuscripts are contemporary with each other, and can be dated to the first half of the fifteenth century. These conclusions echo earlier observations, but confirm them at a much more rigorous level. As the title of the conference makes clear, the map is a forgery, but the investigations of this team promise to provide a comprehensive scientific understanding of the forgery. There are still believers in the authenticity of the map, but, like climate change deniers and moon-landing deniers, they have a faith that is stronger than the evidence.

CHAPTER 4

ICELAND AND THE DISCOVERY OF GREENLAND

In the eighth century the Norse began to migrate from their homelands in Scandinavia to areas to the east, south, and west. Migration normally took the form of a sequence that began with coastal raids, followed by occupation, settlement and colonization. The motive for coastal raids was clearly pillage, but the motive for settlement and colonization is less clear. There was abundant land suitable for farming in Scandinavia, and as recent historians such as Arnved Nedkvitne have shown, there is no evidence for the traditional view that a burgeoning population required new land. Other factors that may have encouraged migration include a wish to connect to European trade networks, an urge to escape from religious conflict associated with the headway made by Christianity in Scandinavia, a need to escape from conflict between warring chieftains, and dispossession occasioned by the gradual centralization of power into regional centres in Scandinavia.

The Norse presence in the Atlantic archipelago was inaugurated by a series of raids on coastal and island targets: the Isle of Portland (789) and the monasteries at Lindisfarne (793), Monkwearmouth-Jarrow (794), and Iona (795). Sources for Ireland in this period are less precise in their dating, but raids appear to have begun on the Antrim coast in the mid 790s, and in 807—the earliest firm date—the western coastal monasteries of Inishmurray (on an island off Sligo) and Roscam (Galway) were attacked. In Wales, Anglesey was attacked c. 853. In the early ninth century Norse settlers arrived in significant numbers in the Northern and Western Isles, and in the Scottish Highlands. By mid-century these settlements had been consolidated into a Norse kingdom, and by the end of the century the royal court had shifted to Dublin. The Norse were expelled from Dublin in 902, but recaptured it fifteen years later. They subsequently invaded northern England, establishing their capital at York (Jorvik). In the opening years of the eleventh century the Norse conquest of England was completed by Sweyn Forkbeard and his son Cnut.

The period of Norse expansion concluded in the mid eleventh century. In the Scandinavian homelands, power became centralized in the kingdoms of Denmark, Norway, and Sweden, and all three adopted Christianity. In the east, trade relations with the Islamic Caliphate in Baghdad were weakened by the rise of the Khazars. In England in 1066, the Norse king Harald was defeated by William of Normandy, the descendant of Norse settlers. In the west, the failure of what may have been a short-lived settlement on the eastern coast of North America and then the Western and Eastern Settlements of Greenland marked the retreat of the Norse to Iceland and Norway. The western expansion under scrutiny in this book will extend from the settlement period in the ninth century to the abandonment of the last Greenland colony in the late fifteenth century.

In the ninth century the expansion of Norse settlements to the west began with the Faroes and extended gradually to Iceland and then Greenland. In the relatively warm climate of the ninth century, these outposts offered farmland and hunting grounds on land and sea. The Norse were not the first settlers in any of these areas, but when they arrived, all three were virtually deserted. The handful of Irish monks that seem to have sought solitude in the Faroes and (probably) Iceland in earlier centuries did not establish permanent communities, not least because they were entirely male.

The Norse settlements were led by chieftains from coastal Norway and the Viking settlements in Scotland and Ireland. This is consistent with recent genomics research, which shows that the present populations of the Faroes and Iceland derive from these areas: the paternal gene pool is predominantly Norse, but the maternal gene pool is predominantly Scottish and Irish. The latter could be explained by the enslavement of female Celts or peaceful intermarriage between Norse settlers and local women.

Details of the first settlements are sketchy, because archaeological evidence is thin, and it is difficult to identify the memorial traces of real people and events in the sagas. Evidence from cereal pollen may imply settlement in the Faroes as early as the fourth century, and there is toponymic evidence (e.g. Paparøkur and Papurshílsur) that Irish monks may have lived there. The presence of sheep on the islands may provide clues to ancient networks. The Latin account of a voyage by St Brendan mentions an island of sheep, and the breed that lived on the Faroese island of Lítla Dímun until 1860 was related to the ancient Soay sheep of St Kilda.

The Norse arrived in the Faroes in the ninth century, and established a parliament, later named the Løgting, at Tinganes. The sagas provide a more elaborate account, but sagas are myths of origin rather than historical documents. The national saga of the Faroes, *Færeyinga Saga*, is an early thirteenth-century narrative that only survives in passages cited in later works. One of these later works is a fourteenth-century compilation of sagas known as *Flateyjarbók*, which contains the opening words of the *Færeyinga Saga*: 'There was a man called Grim Kamban, and he was the first person to live in the Faroes' (*Madr er nefnndr Grimr kamban hann bygde fystr Færeyiar*). The byname Kamban seems to derive from the Gaelic *camb*, meaning 'crooked' (as in Campbell, 'crooked mouth'), which implies that he came from the Norse settlements in Ireland or Scotland. This fleshing out of the name is not meant to imply that Grim was an historical figure, but rather that he was endowed with an implied background. There is no statue of Grim, even in the village of Funningar (Eysturoy), which is said to be where he first landed, but he has been pictured on a postage stamp (on which his name in Faroese is Grímur) (Fig. 4.1).

The next step westward was to Iceland. Again, early settlement is imperfectly understood, and archaeology has thrown up a few teasers, including four Roman coins from the third century CE (from sites in eastern and southern Iceland) and a Roman cup made in the second century CE (from the island of Viðey, near Reykjavík). Such artefacts are not evidence of a Roman presence. They were found with Norse deposits, which implies that they were brought by the Norse during the medieval period. Why they would have owned such things is a mystery. The presence of Irish monks is better attested. The twelfth-century chronicle known as *Íslendingabók* explains that when the Norse arrived, 'there were already Christians, whom the Norse call *papar*' (*Þá váru hér menn kristnir, þeir er Norðmenn kalla Papa*). There is some place-name evidence to support this contention, and a cave at Kverkarhellier,

Fig. 4.1 Stamp depicting Grímur

on a farm in southern Iceland, offers hints of early monastic settlement.

As in the Faroes, there is a mythical founder of Iceland. *Landnámabók* (*landnám* is 'land-taking'), which is known in English as the *Book of Settlements*, attributes the discovery of Iceland to Naddod (Norse: *Naddoðr*), an early Norse settler in the Faroes. Naddod is said to have lost his way while sailing from Norway to the Faroes, and to have made landfall in eastern Iceland near what is now the town of Reyðarfjörður. He named the newly discovered island Snæland ('snowland'). There is some evidence for the historicity of a man called Naddod—the ogham inscriptions on the edges of a ninth- or tenth-century stone cross slab from Bressay, in Shetland, (now on display in the National Museum of Scotland) record the name of a woman called Ann Naddodsdottir—but there is no link to the discovery of Iceland.

The account in *Landnámabók* goes on to recount the legend of Floki Vilgerdarson, who was led by a raven to the west of Iceland, and of Ingolf Arnarson, who is said to have established a farm in what is now Reykjavík. The settlement period in Iceland is traditionally said to have begun in 874 and extended until 930. During these years much of the land tractable to farming became occupied. There was no government beyond the rule of chieftains in the areas in which they held sway. In 930 the chieftains established a national assembly, the Althing (*Alþingi*), at Þingvellir. This act inaugurated the Commonwealth, during which Christianity was adopted, probably in 999 or 1000. In 1262 Iceland submitted to the crown of Norway, and it remained subject to Norway or Denmark until it regained independence in 1944.

Among the early quasi-historical settlers was Eirik Thorvaldsson, known as Eirik the Red (Norse: *Eiríkr hinn rauði*), who is said in the sagas and the *Book of Settlements* to have been the first European to explore and then settle Greenland. A chieftain with that name seems likely to have existed, but it is hard to be confident about which of the legends with which he is associated have a basis in historical fact.

The literary sources say that Eirik was the son of Thorvald Asvaldsson, who had been exiled from Norway in the 970s for manslaughter and moved to western Iceland, bringing with him his son Eirik. The good land was largely taken, so the family settled in Drangar, a hardscrabble site on the rugged Hornstrandir Peninsula (in north-west Iceland), which was abandoned by its last human inhabitants in the 1950s. The family farmed until Eirik's father died. Eirik married a woman called Thjodhild Jorundardottir, who came from Vatn, in the Haukadalur valley, which extends inland from Breiðafjörður, a substantial bay in the west of Iceland. Her stepfather gave Eirik a smallholding on the edge of his property; this farm became known as Eiriksstaðir. Eirik and Thjodhild had two sons, Leif Eirikson (Leif the Lucky) and Thorstein Eirikson. Two other children, Thorvald Eirikson and Freydis Eiriksdottir, seem to have had a different mother, of whom nothing is recorded. All four children feature in the narratives of voyages to lands to the west of Greenland.

Eirik became embroiled in a dispute with his neighbours. It is not clear what started the quarrel—possibly grazing rights—but the consequences were violent. Eirik's slaves were accused of deliberately starting a landslide that fell on the farm of a neighbour called Valthjof. One of Valthjof's relatives, a man called Eyjolf who lived in the farm across the valley from Eiriksstaðir, murdered the slaves; Eirik, in turn, murdered Eyjolf. His punishment was exile from the Haukadalur valley. He moved to Breiðafjörður, where he lent his house-pillars (*setstokkar*, the posts that divided the Norse house into three living spaces) to a man called Thorgest. Eirik then established a farm (again called Eiríksstaðir) on the island of Oxney, and asked for the return of his house-pillars. Thorgest refused, so Eirik went to collect them by force. In the skirmish that followed, two of Thorgest's sons were among those killed. Eirik and his companions were banished for three years by the local assembly (*Þórsnesþing*). Eirik could not return to Norway, and so decided to spend the three years exploring the land to the west that had been sighted by his kinsman Gunnbjorn Ulfsson a century earlier.

The precise location of the first Eiriksstaðir is not specified in *Eiríks saga rauða* (the *Saga of Eirik the Red*), which simply says that Eirik was a man from Breiðafjörðr (modern Icelandic: Breiðafjörður). The site now identified as his farmstead is not attested in any written source before 1731, when it first appears in a land register. The ruins were first excavated in 1895, then again in 1938 and finally in 1997–2000. Current thinking is that the ruins represent a farm that was inhabited for ten to twenty years in the tenth century. If Eirik was an historic figure, then these ruins have a reasonable claim to be the most likely site of his smallholding. In the hope that this might be true, a conjectural reconstruction of the farmhouse based on the surviving ground plan has been built on the site, and a local resident in the guise of a polite Viking tells the story of Eirik, with special reference to the discovery of America by his son Leif Eirikson, who was born at this farm.

In the sagas Eirik commands some respect, but by modern standards he was a serial killer, so it is perhaps unsurprising that he is not celebrated as a national hero in a country remarkable for its eirenic tendencies. There is no statue of Eirik in Iceland, and the floor in the National Museum dedicated to the early history of Iceland makes no mention of Eirik or the Greenland colonies. Perhaps this is an aspect of Iceland's efforts to dissociate itself from Denmark, its former colonial master. Eirik's son Leif has slightly more visibility, but not in the National Museum, and indeed not at the initiative of the people of Iceland. In 1930 a sculpture competition was held in the USA to mark the 1000th anniversary of the founding of Iceland's national assembly, the Alþingi. First Prize was awarded to Stirling Calder's statue of Leif, which now stands in front of Iceland's national cathedral in Reykjavík (Fig. 4.2). An inscription on the back reads 'Leifr

Fig. 4.2 Leif Eirikson statue, Reykjavík

Eiricsson son of Iceland discoverer of Vinland the United States of America to the people of Iceland on the one thousandth anniversary of the Althing AD 1930'. Second prize was awarded to the Icelandic sculptor Nína Sæmundsson (said to be a descendant of Eirik and Leif), again for a statue of Leif, which now stands in Eiríksstaðir (Fig. 4.3).

Fig. 4.3 Leif Eirikson statue, Eiríksstaðir

It would seem that Leif features more prominently in the American historical imagination than in the country of his birth. In 2000 the United States Mint issued two Leif Ericson millennium commemorative coins to mark Leif's voyage to America: an American silver dollar and an Icelandic silver 1,000 króna. The American coin describes Leif as 'Founder of the New World'.

Such sentiments are ideologically charged. The notion that Leif was the founder of the New World assumes not only that the native peoples of the Americas played no founding role, but also that Greenland is not part of the New World. As a feisty sign headed 'Greenland as part of North America' in the National Museum of Greenland explains, it is natural for

many Greenlanders, especially the younger ones who have not experienced the colonial period, to feel a strong affinity with their kinsmen to the West. They speak the same language and have the same cultural background as the Inuit in Canada and Alaska, a common inheritance passed down over thousands of years before the white man's "discoveries". Looked at in this way, we should perhaps regard Erik the Red as the first "white" man to discover this territory, rather than his son Leif Eriksson, who in the wake of his father's exploits took a "day trip" from the colonised area of Greenland to the American continent.

This is a robust perspective that is hard to find in traditional American and European accounts of the Norse crossing of the North Atlantic.

The sagas and the Icelandic *Book of Settlements* (*Landnámabók*) present new discoveries in a fixed pattern: a ship is blown to the west, and an unknown land is sighted. Landfall is followed by investigation to assess the prospects for settlement, then settlers arrive, land is claimed (*landnám*), and the territory is colonized. The account of the European discovery of Greenland in the *Book of Settlements* conforms to this pattern. Early in the tenth century, according to the *Book of Settlements*, Gunnbjörn Ulfsson was blown off course in a storm while sailing from Norway to Iceland, and saw skerries off the coast of a new land. He did not land, but the skerries were named after him (Gunnbjarnarsker). The location of these islands is not specified and cannot now be identified. Indeed, it is possible, if the story has some basis in fact, that they were an Arctic mirage.

In about 978, the first intentional voyage to Greenland is said to have been undertaken by Snæbjörn Galti, who explored the inhospitable eastern coast. He was killed by a member of his crew before he could return to Iceland. Both Gunnbjörn and Snæbjörn were said to have been related to Eirik, and their families lived in the same area as his homestead, so it is possible that his decision to sail west to Greenland to serve his three-year exile from Iceland was informed by some inkling of what to expect. Eirik sailed from Snæfellsjökull, a highly visible mountain on the tip of the peninsula in westernmost Iceland, which was used by generations of sailors as a navigational marker. The Norse were adept at sailing along lines of latitude and so would have sailed due west from Snæfellsjökull to the coast of Greenland. There were no charts: navigation was primarily by sun and star, supplemented by gradually accumulated knowledge of currents and ice. In the case of the sun, Norse seafarers seem to have used a form of sun compass to calculate the sun's declination. A notched wooden disc now on display in the National Museum of Denmark seems to bear witness to the use of such instruments.

On arriving on Greenland's east coast, which offers few opportunities for landfall, Eirik would have sailed south-west, rounded Cape Farewell (Greenlandic: Nunap Isua; Danish: Cap Farvel) at the southern extremity of Greenland, and sailed north-west to the clement fjords that were to become the first settlement area. In 986, when he was allowed to return to Iceland, Eirik recruited settlers, who sailed west in a fleet of twenty-five ships. Only fourteen ships reached Greenland, with some 500 settlers; the other eleven ships either sank or turned back to Iceland. There were two principal areas of settlement. The larger settlement, in the southwestern fjords, initially had some 200 farms; it was known as the Eastern Settlement (Eystribyggð). The smaller settlement, further north along the west coast in the area of what is now Nuuk, had fewer than 100 farms; it was known as the Western Settlement (Vestribyggð). There is archaeological evidence of a small third settlement, not attested in the saga literature, consisting of about twenty farms; it is now known (in

Danish rather than Old Norse) as the Middle Settlement (Mellembygden).

The two settlements were each spread over a large area. In contrast to later colonial settlements in America, there were in the first instance no villages, but rather scattered farmsteads. Settlers in America were making inroads into a land already occupied, but the Norse were alone in southern Greenland when the settlements were being established. According to the written sources, eleven chieftains established farmsteads along the fjords in the Eastern Settlement, on the south-west coast of Greenland. Each chieftain's farm, known in Danish as a 'named farm' (*navnegård*), typically accommodated on its land one or more small farms run by peasant farmers.

Many of the fjords were named after chieftains in the sagas and chronicles. As the *Book of Settlements* explains,

> Eirik the Red then took Eirikfjord and lived in Brattahlid, and Leif his son followed him. These men who went out with Eirik took land in Greenland: Herjof took Herjolfjord and lived in Herjolfsnes, Ketill took Ketilsfjord, Hrafn took Hrafnsfjord, Sölvi took Sölvadal, Helgi Thorbrandsson took Alftafjord, Thorbjorn Glora took Siglufjord, Einar took Einarsfjord, Hafgrim took Hafgrimsfjord and the district of Vatna, Arnlaug took Arnlaugsfjord, and some travelled to the Western Settlement.

> [*Eiríkr rauði nam síðan Eiríksfjörð ok bjó í Brattahlíð, en Leifr son hans eptir hann. Þessir menn námu lönd á Grænalandi, er þá fóru út með Eiríki: Herjólfur Herjólfsfjörð; hann bjó á Herjólfsnesi, Ketill Ketilsfjörð, Hrafn Hrafnsfjörð, Sölvi Sölvadal, Helgi Þorbrandsson Álptafjörð, Þorbjörn glóra Siglufjörð, Einarr Einarsfjörð, Hafgrímr Hafgrímsfjörð ok Vatnahverfi, Arnlaugr Arnlaugsfjörð, en sumir fóru til vestri bygðar*]

When Denmark began to colonize Greenland in the eighteenth century, the process of matching Inuit place names with the place names in the Norse sources began in earnest, so, for the Danish colonizers, Tunulliarfik became Eiriksfjord, Narssap Sarqa became Herjolfsfjord, Tasermiut became Ketilsfjord, and Igaliku became Einarsfjord, thus hardening the names of semi-historical chieftains into the historical eponyms of real places.

'Some travelled to the Western Settlement' (*sumir fóru til vestri bygðar*). It is not clear who the 'some' might have been, but the absence of names might allow a cautious inference to the effect that the Western Settlement was settled by peasant farmers rather than chieftains. Arnved Nedkvitne has argued persuasively that the Western Settlement may have been administered from Brattahlid through Eirik's son Thorstein, who lived on a farm (Lysufjord) in the Western Settlement, and may have functioned 'as a representative of the Brattahlid clan in the Western Settlement'. He goes on to argue that 'judicial protection for peasants in the Western Settlement may have been given by the chieftain at Brattahlid and organized from Thorstein's farm'. It therefore seems possible that the societal structures in the Western Settlement differed very considerably from those in the Eastern Settlement, where the chieftains were able to exercise their authority directly.

The society that the Norse created in these settlements was to endure for centuries. The next chapter will describe the society created by the Norse Greenlanders, and consider why it came to an end after 500 years.

CHAPTER 5

NORSE GREENLAND

The medieval Norse had a settled presence in Greenland for almost five centuries, from the late tenth century until the mid fifteenth century. The beginnings of the settlements are shrouded in the mists and myths of the sagas, and the final disappearance of the settlements is unrecorded in any form. Accounts of the initial settlement therefore often take the form of literal readings of the sagas, and accounts of the last days take the form of untrammelled speculation, sometimes cast as an unresolved mystery, sometimes as an ecological parable, and sometimes as the final stage before emigration to the North American mainland.

For the centuries between these events, however, there is an abundance of archaeological remains that yields evidence of how the Norse Greenlanders lived. There is, however, little written evidence, and most of what survives was written by outsiders from Iceland. The settlers spoke a dialect now known as Greenlandic Norse, which is attested in scores of runic inscriptions. The find-spots of some of the Norse inscriptions give some sense of the geographical limits of the colonists' travels, but there is no written account of the life of the settlements.

In the sagas and chronicles, the central figures are Norse, because the principal listeners to the sagas were Norse. There are, however, other characters of Gaelic, Germanic, and Sami origin. Genetic evidence from the Norse colonies in the North Atlantic supports this notion of a multi-ethnic society in Greenland. The Norse had established settlements in Scotland and Ireland, and they enslaved local people of Gaelic ancestry. The genetic inheritance of the present people of Iceland indicates, with respect to the founding generation, that at least 20 per cent of the paternal gene pool and at 60 per cent of the maternal gene pool was Gaelic. This must have been true of the Greenlandic Norse as well. Indeed, there is evidence of a member of my own clan being present. In the course of a dig conducted in 1976–7, excavators at Nipaatsoq, near Sandnes in the Western Settlement, found a small silver shield that seems to have been manufactured locally, probably on the farm where it was found (an unworked piece of silver was found nearby) (Fig. 5.1). The shield, now on display in the Greenland National Museum in Nuuk, has a coat of arms divided into eight segments: in the language of heraldry, it is a 'gyronny of eight', which remains the basis of Campbell heraldry up to the present day. The coat of arms first appears on the shield of Colin Campbell (Cailean Mór Caimbeul) in 1296, and remained in this form until the sixteenth century. The most important piece of corroborative evidence is a leather knife sheath now kept in storage in the Museum of London (A3664) (Fig. 5.2). The impressed decoration on the shield includes a virtually identical shield (just below a device associated with the Fitzwalter family). The date of the sheath, in the view of the Museum of London, is thirteenth century, but the presence of the Campbell coat of arms makes a fourteenth-century date more likely. It would seem that the person who made the shield in fourteenth-century Greenland may have been a Campbell. The Campbells were not a seafaring clan and so

Fig. 5.1 Campbell shield, Greenland National Museum, Nuuk

Fig. 5.2 Leather knife sheath, Museum of London

would not have travelled under their own sails, but Scots seem to have been numbered among the settlers. If I were to imitate the eccentric claims of those who assert that their ancestors 'discovered' America, I could argue that the reason that the Campbell who fashioned the shield disappeared from the record in Greenland was because he or she went off to discover America. Claims founded on ancestral links are tendentious, and should not be taken seriously.

The first settlers in the Norse settlements were hunters, fishermen, and stock farmers. The balance between these activities has long been a subject of debate. It is certainly possible that the ivory trade was a motive for the initial settlements, because walrus could be hunted for their tusks. There is abundant evidence from archaeological and literary sources (notably the mid thirteenth-century *Konungs skuggsjá*, an educational text known in English as the *King's Mirror* and in Latin as *Speculum regale*) that the Norse Greenlanders hunted animals such as caribou, whale, seal, wildfowl, and bear for food, and in some cases export. The principal meat eaten on the farms was seal. Seal oil was also used for lighting and heating, and seal skin for clothing. Similarly, whale teeth were used to fashion knife handles, and whale bones were shaped into tools for axes, sledges, and weaving. There was also inshore and fjord fishing for cod and Greenland halibut and freshwater fishing for Arctic char, though saltwater fish was gradually displaced by seal in the Greenlanders' diet. In the Western Settlement walrus could be hunted for meat and for the export of ivory.

The Greenland settlements had good pastures and meadows, but grains could not ripen in the short growing season. Grazing animals were therefore fed on grass. The settlers brought with them a range of domestic animals, principally cattle, but also sheep, pigs, goats, horses, dogs, and cats. Cattle were grazed in communal upland pastures during the five warmest months and confined to sheds in the winter, feeding on the grasses grown close to the farmhouses on fertilized fields. This same pattern is in evidence today in the sheep farms on the sites of the former settlements. The *King's Mirror* claims that some chieftains experimented with crops such as rye and barley, but these grains did not yet exist in short-season varieties, and there are few places with sufficient warmth for such crops to ripen. It seems improbable that there was bread, but the quern stones found on several farms may suggest otherwise.

The farms in the Eastern Settlement were generally inland, often near the heads of fjords. The notable exception to this generalization is Ikigait, which has been identified with the Norse place name Herjolfsnes (Norse: Herjolfsnæs); it was the southernmost farmstead in the Eastern Settlement. The buildings were constructed near the mouth of a fjord, facing the open sea. This may imply that the site was intended as a trading centre for European ships. The fact that Herjolfsnes is the only Greenland settlement shown on the Skálholt Map strengthens this hypothesis. The graveyard at Herjolfses has yielded an immense amount of Norse clothing, made locally but based on European designs. I shall return to this clothing in the context of the end of the Greenland settlements.

There is evidence that the Greenland Norse exported hides from domestic animals, marine mammals (chiefly sealskins, but also whale products), and land mammals (probably ermine and Arctic fox, though in small numbers). Occasionally, live polar bears and birds of prey (hawks and falcons) were exported. The most valuable export, especially for the first three centuries, was walrus. The fourteenth-century *Króka-Refs Saga* records that a man called Bard (Barð), sailing to Greenland in the service of Harald Hardrada (Norse: Haraldr Sigurðarson or Haraldr Harðráði), the eleventh-century Norse king, returned with a cargo of walrus ropes, walrus tusks and skins, and presented the king with a polar bear, a walrus skull (with its valuable tusks), and a chessboard made from walrus ivory. King Harald was certainly an historical figure: he was a claimant to the throne of England, and died in 1066 at the Battle of Stamford Bridge. The story of Bard may be a legend, but the notion of polar bear and walrus products from Greenland being presented to the King is entirely plausible. Rope made from walrus skin was prized for its strength and so was used on royal warships. The Lewis chessmen, mostly now in the British Museum, were probably made from Greenlandic walrus ivory and whales' teeth.

The principal import needed by the Norse settlers was wood, which they used for the construction of ships and boats; timber was also used generously in houses. Some wood was imported from Scandinavia, and driftwood that the Transpolar Drift Stream had brought from the rivers of Siberia was widely used. The question arises whether Norse settlers crossed the Davis Strait to what is now Labrador to harvest wood. At present there is neither archaeological evidence in Labrador nor any medieval wood in Greenland that can be shown to have come from Labrador. There is, however, an entry in the Icelandic Annals which describes the arrival in Iceland in 1347 of a small ship that had sailed from Greenland to Markland, had lost its anchor, and had drifted to Iceland. The entry does not say why the ship had been in Markland, nor is there any intimation that such voyages were usual or unusual, but it seems entirely possible that the reason for the voyage was the harvesting of timber from Labrador's forests. And while nothing in the sagas can be securely taken as fact, a thirteenth-century interpolation in *Saga of the Greenlanders* claims that both Leif Eirikson and Thorfinn Karlsefni brought timber back from Markland. It seems reasonable to infer that the Norse did indeed travel to Labrador for timber, but it would not be safe to assume that such voyages took place throughout the centuries of Norse settlement. Perhaps they did, but it is also possible that changing conditions in the fourteenth century occasioned an increase in the number of voyages.

The second most important import was iron. The Norse were certainly capable of producing bog iron, and they did so in Scandinavia, Iceland, and at L'Anse aux Meadows. The difficulty in Greenland was a lack of fuel to smelt the bog ore in an oven, and no evidence has been discovered to suggest that bog ore was smelted in Greenland. Instead, the Norse settlers imported iron bloom, which was then forged into tools, knives, nails, ship rivets, and weapons at smithies on the principal Greenlandic farms. A lack of fuel for smelting would not have been a problem in Labrador, so one might cautiously wonder whether work conducted there might have included the construction of ships and boats, using bog iron bloom brought from Greenland to forge rivets.

The formal institution of the state did not exist in Greenland before 1261. Power was vested in the chieftains, who exercized their authority in what was a loosely constituted free state. Civil society was in the first instance regulated by oral customary law through the Althing at Gardar (now Igaliku). In 1261 the Greenland Norse submitted to the Norwegian crown, and as part of the kingdom of

Norway, began to pay taxes (and fines for manslaughter) to the King of Norway. In 1274 King Magnus VI (Magnús Hákonarson) produced a new code of law for his realm, after which he became known as Magnus the Law-Amender (Magnús lagabœtir). This new body of law applied in Greenland, but seems to have been used in modified form by the Althing at Gardar in its resolution of disputes relating to church regulations, criminal law, land law, and commercial law. Whether this Greenlandic law was oral or written is not known, but it seems likely that a written copy arrived in Greenland at some point, so the law-speaker (lögmaðr) may have worked from a written text. The Althing convened at an unknown location in Gardar, probably close to the track (now known as Kongevejen—the King's Way) that leads up to the crossing to the next fjord. All offences, ranging from disputes with the Church to murder arising from blood feuds, were treated as private conflicts. As in Iceland's Althing, disputants stayed in 'booths' (Norse: búðir; see Glossary) near the court during the proceedings. They arrived with entourages of armed men, and intimidation of juries could be a problem, but disputes were resolved.

The most powerful institution in Norse Greenland was the Church. Most of the earliest settlers were pagans, but it is likely that some were Christians. The Book of Settlements and the Saga of the Greenlanders record that a Norse-speaking Christian from the Hebrides who sailed with Herjolf (one of the original settlers) composed the Hafgerðingadrápa ('Lay of the Sea Mountains'), of which one surviving fragment is a prayer:

> I ask the sinless Master of Monks for a safe voyage
> May the heavenly Lord hold his hand over me
> [Mínar bid ek at munka reyni meinalausan farar beina,
> heidis haldi harar foldar hallar drottinnyfirmer stalli]

This Norse Hebridean may not be an historical figure, but the notion of a Christian among the earliest settlers is not fanciful. As the earliest churches appear to be approximately contemporary with the earliest farmhouses, it seems that the settlers became Christians at a very early stage.

The first Christian church mentioned in literary sources is said to have been built by Thjodhild Jörundardottir (the Christian wife of Eirik the Red) at Brattahlid. In chapter 2, I explained that in the *Saga of Eirik the Red*, Leif Eirikson came home to Brattahlid and preached Christianity to the household. Leif's father Eirik was not keen on the new religion, but his mother Thjodhild converted (and severed marital relations with the resolutely pagan Eirik) and built a small church. Brattahlid is popularly identified with Qassiarsuk (though there is a contested alternative candidate at Qinngua, at the northern end of the fjord). In Qassiarsuk the remains of an early church have been found and a reconstruction built nearby (Fig. 5.3). The archaeologist who excavated the church in 1961 confidently identified it as Thjodhild's church, so hardening the fanciful story of Leif's Christianizing mission in the saga into fact. Most of the early burials were articulated skeletons buried on an east–west axis, and so were Christian; some were simply collections of disarticulated bones, for which one possible explanation is that they were Christian reburials of bones retrieved from a pagan mound. Whether or not the building is Thjodhild's church cannot be ascertained, but it seems likely that this is the first Christian church and churchyard to be constructed in the Americas.

Most early churches in Greenland were rectangular structures with an outer casing of turf, a design with clear antecedents in Iceland and Norway. There are, however, at least seven small, early

Fig. 5.3 Reconstruction of Thjodhild's church, Qassiarsuk

churches that have circular or ovoid walls or dykes encompassing the surrounding burial grounds; such walls were common in the Celtic parts of Britain and Ireland occupied by the Norse, and in Celtic-influenced Iceland and the Faroes. This apparent origin of Greenlandic structures opens the possibility that early Christianity in Greenland had Celtic elements. Several other churches point to another possible influence: an early church at Gardar (preceding the cathedral), and another with a smaller version of the same design at Sandnes (in the Western Settlement), for example, share many features, such as a west wall made of wood and other walls of stone. Their most striking feature is that the square-ended chancels are narrower than the naves, which is a feature of early Anglo-Saxon churches, such as the seventh-century church in Escomb (County Durham). Arnved Nedkvitne has argued that these churches were built by English missionaries who were among the first priests in Greenland. A pendant cross found at Hvalsey (now temporarily misplaced in the museum at Qaqortoq) is apparently made of English pewter. This cross could be a trade product, but it could also be a fragmentary piece of evidence of an English presence in Norse Greenland. Evidence from architecture and artefacts is tantalizing, but not sufficiently strong to warrant firm conclusions.

Before the parish system was implemented, churches were associated with farms, and so functioned as household chapels. Some had full-time priests, and others called on local itinerant priests to conduct services. There is no evidence of episcopal oversight before the early twelfth century. The journey of the semi-mythical Bishop Eirik Gnupsson (see Chapter 2) is dated 1112. Solid evidence emerges in 1124, when a Greenland diocese was created with the episcopal seat at Gardar. Arnald was consecrated as bishop in Lund (then part of Denmark) and arrived in Gardar in 1126. During his long tenure of office (until c. 1150) he oversaw the first stage of the construction of the Cathedral of St Nicholas and the episcopal manor at Gardar. It is not known why Gardar was chosen as the seat of the bishop. Perhaps a high-status chieftain occupied the site and hosted the assembly, so Gardar had already become the principal seat of authority in Greenland, but it is also possible that the presence of a cathedral conferred on Gardar a national standing, and so it became the seat of the annual assembly. Archaeology may in due course yield answers to such questions.

In 1886 the cathedral and manor were identified with the ruins at Igaliku (Fig. 5.4). Many identifications of Norse place names with Greenlandic sites are dubious, but this identification has proved to be uniquely solid.

Fig. 5.4 Ruins of the episcopal manor at Gardar (now Igaliku)

The most recent (2007) archaeological analysis of the cathedral concludes that a twelfth-century Romanesque building constructed from local sandstone was expanded in the thirteenth century into a substantial cruciform church furnished with a bell tower and tinted glass. Other buildings associated with the see include a palace with a ceremonial hall that could seat at least fifty guests, two byres that could accommodate 100 cattle, and a large tithe barn. A herd of 100 cattle required substantial grazing in the summer and grass grown on manured fields for fodder in the winter months. The dividends of several centuries of fertilization are still apparent in the many vegetable gardens in the village. Water for fields, animals, and human residents was supplied by an elaborate irrigation system that drew water from reservoirs in the hills above the settlement.

The arrival of a bishop integrated the Greenlandic church into the ecclesiastical hierarchy. The diocese of Gardar was part of the archiepiscopal province of Bremen until 1104, Lund until 1153, and Nidaros (now Trondheim) thereafter. The vast province of Nidaros had eleven dioceses, including the Faroes, the Icelandic dioceses of Hólar and Skálholt, the Northern Isles (Orkney and Shetland), and the Western Isles (the Hebrides and the Isle of Man). The parish system was introduced in the diocese of Gardar, with twelve parishes in the Eastern Settlement and either three or four (sources are inconsistent) in the Western Settlement. The total number of farm churches is not known, but to date twenty-one parish or farm churches have been found. The best preserved of these churches is Hvalsey, in the Eastern Settlement. The surviving church was built in the fourteenth century, but its foundations rest in part on grave stones associated with an earlier church on the site. It was in Hvalsey that the last recorded events in the history of the Greenland Norse occurred in 1407 and 1408. In 1407 a young man called Kolgrim was found guilty of having seduced a married woman through black magic (*svarta kuonstrum*). Adultery could be overlooked, but *maleficium* (causing harm through the use of magic) was an offence under canon law, so Kolgrim was sentenced by a local court to be burnt at the stake. The following year, on 16 September 1408, there was a society wedding in Hvalsey Church when two high-born Icelanders were married. Thereafter the written record ceases.

In addition to the parish churches, the diocese of Gardar also had two monasteries: a community of Augustinian Canons Regular for men in Ketilsfjord (now Tasermiut Fjord), and a Benedictine convent for women in Siglufjord (now Uunartoq Fjord), each with a church. The Canons Regular were neither monks nor friars, but rather priests living in community, and so able to celebrate mass in other churches in the settlement. Neither

Fig. 5.5 Hvalsey Church, Qaqortukulooq

monastery has been identified with certainty, though archaeologists have tentatively associated them with specific sites. Nuns were able to care for the sick in the settlement, probably with the use of the hot springs on Uunartoq island. The identity and origins of the canons and nuns are unknown, but both orders were represented in Iceland (where an abbot of the Canons Regular became the nation's first saint) and Norway (where there were two Benedictine nunneries).

There is little evidence to judge literacy among lay people in Norse Greenland. The source of literacy was the church, and surviving inscriptions bear mute witness to the ability to read and write amongst those close to the church. The language of the church in Greenland was Latin, and a few inscriptions (sometimes in roman letters, sometimes in runic) testify to some competence in that language. When Nidaros (now Trondheim) became the seat of an archbishop in 1153, schools for the education of clergy were established at the cathedrals in many or all of the eleven dioceses. The discovery in 2012 of seven new runic inscriptions at Gardar (now in the Greenland National Museum in Nuuk) provided evidence that such a school may have existed there. One is a lump of wood inscribed on one side with a prayer that can be transcribed as [*benedi*]*ctus fructus ventris tui* ('blessed is the fruit of your womb'). A second is a wooden stick, possibly the arm of a cross, with a fragment of the opening words of the Mass translated into Norse, which can be transliterated *I namna föður ok*... ('In the name of the Father and...'). Inscriptions that represent a personal name or an identification of what is being written, such as the word *rúnar* ('runes') written in runes on a shaped piece of wood, have been interpreted plausibly as the work of learners in a school.

Arnald, who arrived in Gardar in 1126, was the first of a line of nine resident bishops. The ninth was Álf, a Benedictine monk who arrived in Gardar in 1368. The annals give four different years in the late 1370s for his date for his death; 1378 seems the most likely. The news of Álf's death did not reach Nidaros until 1384, by which time the archbishop had died and the Roman Curia chose to prefer a Danish candidate called Henricus to the Norwegian nominated by the cathedral chapter in Nidaros. Henricus was translated to Orkney in 1394, and in the same year, the right to appoint bishops of Gardar reverted from Nidaros to Rome. Thereafter a succession of thirteen non-resident bishops was appointed to the see of Gardar. The last of these appointments (until the see was revived in 2001) was in 1519, when the Observant Franciscan Vincent Peter Kampe was appointed as Bishop of Gardar. He seems to have remained in office until 1537, when Lutheranism was imposed by decree on Norway and its North

Atlantic colonies and the Catholic Church lost all its possessions. Thereafter there was no point in appointing bishops to Gardar. It seems overwhelmingly likely that the Greenland settlements had vanished by 1537, but it is not known at what point Rome and Nidaros lost contact with the church in Greenland.

There was no bishop resident in Greenland after 1378, but the church carried on, because there were still priests in residence acting as vicars general. The final record of a functioning church concerns the wedding at Hvalsey on 16 September 1408. The following year, on 19 April, the Gardar officialis (the priest authorized to act in the bishop's absence) Eindridi Andresson and the priest Pall Hallvardsson attested that the correct procedures had been carried out and that banns had been read in the cathedral on the three Sundays before the wedding. This letter, which survives in a seventeenth-century transcription, is the only document known to have been written in Norse Greenland, and the last written evidence of the Norse church in Greenland.

At an early point in the history of the settlements, the Norse discovered that they were not the only human inhabitants of Greenland, and, probably for the first time, native Europeans met native North Americans.

Greenland had three founding peoples: the Tuniit, the Norse, and the Thule; none of the three now exists, though the Thule peoples have Inuit descendants who now live in Greenland. It is customary to speak of the Greenland Norse as 'colonists', as though they were claiming territory on behalf of a foreign power; 'settlers' is a less ideologically charged term. The Tuniit and Thule were migratory groups who did not form permanent settlements, but they used sites repeatedly.

The Norse settled in what was apparently an uninhabited land. There had, however, been an intermittent human presence in Greenland for millennia. The first arrivals were the Tuniit people. The archaeological term for the Tuniit is Palaeo-Eskimo. This may be misleading, in that it is unlikely that they spoke an Eskimo language and they had no progeny: they were not the ancestors of the Inuit. The Tuniit had over the course of several centuries traversed what is now Canada from their original home on both sides of the Bering Strait. The earliest known settlers in Greenland were the Tuniit people known as the Saqqaq culture, who lived in scattered communities on the west and south-east coasts from c. 2500 BCE to c. 800 BCE. Their contemporaries, known as Independence Culture I, lived in the far north and north-east. They were succeeded, initially in the same northerly area, by the people variously known as Independence II or Greenlandic Dorset.

The Dorset people were the last of the Tuniit groups in the Eastern Arctic. In Canada, around Ungava Bay, a continuous history can be documented from c. 900 BCE to c. 1500 CE. In Greenland there is a gap in dateable material from c. 200 to c. 1100; then there is a second documented period ('Late Dorset') from c. 1100 to c. 1300. The 900-year gap in the archaeological record may mean that the Dorset were absent, or simply that traces of their presence have not been found. The aphorism 'absence of evidence is not evidence of absence' obtains, so we simply do not know whether Greenland had been continuously inhabited or whether it was inhabited when the Norse arrived. At the end of the period, there is no evidence of a Dorset presence in Greenland after the thirteenth century.

The final migration to Greenland from the west was the arrival of the neo-Eskimo group known as the Thule people, whose cultural and biological descendants are the Inuit of our own time. The Thule originated in northern Alaska c. 1000 CE, and in the course of the next two centuries reached the Eastern Arctic, arriving in Greenland c. 1200, and gradually moving south along both coasts as climate change forced the ringed seals south. By the fifteenth century they seem to have eschewed the high Arctic in favour of southern sites, but a new wave of Thule migrants came to north-west Greenland in the eighteenth century.

The Norse arrived in Greenland c. 985, and stayed for almost 500 years. Late Dorset occupation is attested from c. 1100–c. 1300; Thule people and their Inuit descendants have been continuously present since 1200. Norse hunting grounds extended ever further north. In 1824 a runestone (now in the National Museum of Denmark) was found in a group of cairns at the highest point of Kingittorsuaq Island, in north-west Greenland. Transcribed from runic characters into the modified Latin alphabet of Icelandic, it has been transcribed as *Erlingur Sigvaðs sonur og baarne Þorðarson og enriði ás son laugardagin fyrir gakndag hloðu varða thessa og ryðu*, which might be translated 'Erling the son of Sigvad and Baarne Thordar's son and Enridi As's son, the Saturday before Rogation Day, raised this cairn and rode'. No year is given, but it must have been carved in the thirteenth century by three hunters who had travelled north in the spring (Rogation Day fell on 25 April). As the Norse hunting grounds edged north, and the Dorset and Thule south, there were inevitably contacts. The *Historia Norwegie*, a short Latin history of Norway from the second half of the twelfth century, explains that,

> North of the settlements of the Norse Greenlanders, hunters have encountered little people whom they call Skrælings. If these people were wounded with Norse weapons, their wounds became white without bleeding, but if the blows were fatal, the blood flowed

heavily. They do not have iron, and instead use walrus teeth as missiles and sharp stones as knives.

[*Trans Viridenses ad aquilonem quidam homunciones a uenatoribus reperi-*
untur, quos Screlinga appellant. Qui dum uiui armis feriuntur, uulnera
eorum absque cruore albescunt, mortuis uero uix cessat sanguis manare. Sed
ferri metallo penitus carent; dentibus cetinis pro missilibus, saxis acutis pro
cultris utuntur]

The date implies that the people encountered by the Norse were Dorset.

The only other known encounter from this period is recorded in the Icelandic Annals for 1379, which describe an attack by skrælings in which eighteen Norse were killed and two Norse boys captured and enslaved. The location of the attack is not recorded, but by 1379 the Western Settlement had been deserted, as had the small Middle Settlement, so the encounter must have taken place in the Eastern Settlement, in the far south of Greenland. This time, the people seem to have been Thule, specifically the people associated with the late Ruin Island phase of Thule culture, and this passage is the earliest evidence that the Thule had travelled the length of Greenland.

Such violent interactions may have existed alongside the peaceful activity of trade. Artefacts of Norse origin have been found on a few Late Dorset sites in Greenland, and in the Thule sites on Ruin Island (1,700 kilometres north of the Western Settlement), and this might point to trade. On the other hand, there is no evidence of barter, though it would clearly have been advantageous to the Norse to secure walrus tusks from Dorset and Thule people, as this was the most lucrative product being exported to Europe. Trade may have taken place in the far north. A Thule site of the Ruin Island type on Ellesmere Island, a short distance across

Smith Sound from Greenland, has yielded iron ship rivets, which would seem to imply the wreck of a Norse ship caught in the ice. The question of the limits of Norse travel beyond Greenland will be considered in chapter 7.

The Norse had a settled presence in Greenland for as long as Europeans have had a continuous presence in what is now the United States (beginning with San Agustín in Florida in 1565). The Norse farmed and hunted for centuries and worshipped in a cathedral and parish churches built in a European idiom. At some point the society that they had built was cut off from European contact, and later abandoned. Why? The notion of a mysterious disappearance arose in the early eighteenth century. The Greenland settlements had never been forgotten in Norway during the centuries when there was no contact, and after the Reformation there were several unrealized plans to convert the Norse Greenlanders to the Lutheran faith and reinstitute a tax regime. In 1536, in the wake of Swedish secession from the Union of Kalmar, a combined Danish-Norwegian kingdom was created, with Copenhagen as its capital. Danes soon began to share the vision of a North Atlantic empire that included Greenland.

Hans Egede was a Danish-Norwegian Lutheran who in 1721 sailed as a 'royal missionary' with a small fleet (three ships) to Greenland, landing near what is now Nuuk. He soon found the ruins of the Western Settlement, but instead of Norse settlers there were Inuit. His missionary endeavours included translating the Lord's Prayer into Kalaallisut (West Greenlandic), adapting to the fact that there was no bread in Greenland by translating the fourth petition as 'give us this day our daily seal'. He knew that there were two Norse settlements in Greenland and assumed correctly that he had found the Western Settlement. He was, however, understandably misled by the assumptions that the Eastern Settlement was on the east coast of Greenland and that a strait allowed it to be reached without rounding Cape Farewell. Eventually he located the Eastern Settlement (where he explored the ruins of Hvalsey Church) and concluded that there were no remaining Norse settlers. Their disappearance was presented as an enigma and has ever since been treated as a Marie Celeste mystery.

The end of the Greenland settlement raises a series of questions that must be repeated for the two evacuations, that of the Western Settlement and that of the Eastern Settlement. When and why did these evacuations occur, and where did the settlers go?

The principal source for the end of the Western Settlement is the 'Description of Greenland' composed c. 1360 by Ivar Bardarson, a priest at Gardar Cathedral who also served as a tax collector. Ivar's 'Description' survives in a seventeenth-century copy of a sixteenth-century manuscript based on a lost original that Ivar had dictated to a scribe; the text seems to contain some interpolations written long after Ivar dictated his account. It is not a forgery, in that it contains detailed information about the Eastern Settlement that clearly comes from a fourteenth-century source, but the account of the Western Settlement should not be assumed to be dispassionate or accurate.

In the final section of the 'Description', Ivar declares in his own voice that

> in the Western settlement there stands a large church called Stensnes Church, which was once the cathedral and the seat of the bishop. Now the Skrælings have destroyed the entire Western Settlement, and all that is left are some feral horses, goats, cattle and sheep. There are no people, either Christian or heathen.

[*vdj Vesterbijgd stander en stuor kircke, som heder Stensnes ircke, then kircke vor en stund domkircke och biscops sedet, nu haffue Skrelinge all Vesterbijgden vdt, tha er ther nog heste, geder, nød och faar, alt vilt, och inthet folck enthen Christen eller heden*].

This information is then repeated with a few extra details in the voice of the scribe

All of this was told to us by Ivar Bardarson the Greenlander, who was for many years the superintendent of the bishop's see at Gardar. He had seen all this, and he was one of those sent by the lawman to deal with the Skrælings in the Western Settlement, in order to expel them from the Settlement. When they arrived, they found nobody, neither Christian nor heathen, only some feral cattle and sheep, and they slaughtered the cattle and sheep for food, as many as could be loaded onto the ships, and then sailed a home with the aforementioned Ivan.

[*Dette alt som forsaugd er sagde oss Iffuer Bardsenn Grønlenndinger, som vor forstander paa biscopsgaarden i Gardum paa Grønland vdj mange aar, ath hand hafde alt dette seet, och hand vor en aff thennom, som vor vdneffnder aff laugmader ath fare till Vesterbijgdt emod the Skrelinge, ath uddriffve the Skrelinge vdaff Vesterbijgd, och tha the komme tiid, tha funde de ingen mand enthen christne eller hedne vden nogit vilt fæ och foer och bespisede sigh aff thet vilt fæ och faar saa megit som skibene kunde bere och seiglede saa, sielff ther met hiem och for^{ne} Iuer vor then med.*]

The repetition is testament to the transmitted nature of the account.

How much of this account is to be believed? Could, for example, the church at Sandnes (Stensnes) once have been a cathedral and the seat of a bishop? No other source makes that suggestion, but the church at Sandnes is a slightly smaller version of the early church at Gardar (the predecessor of Gardar Cathedral), so it is possible that Ivan's claim is a faint memory of a time when the farms of Sandnes and Gardar, which are linked in the sagas because they were occupied by the children of Eirik the Red, hosted the most important churches in their respective settlements.

Ivar's account is undated, as is his visit to the Western Settlement. He lived in Greenland intermittently from 1341 until c. 1360, but was in the papal court in Avignon in 1344, and may not have returned to Greenland until 1354 The documentary record is fragmentary, and the visit could have taken place any time during those nineteen years. Why did Ivar see neither Norse nor Thule? One possibility is that he wasn't looking hard enough. There may have been Thule living nearby (on Kangeq Island), but they were few in number and may not have been inclined to introduce themselves to an armed party of visiting Norse. And if the real purpose of Ivar's visit was to collect taxes and tithes, the Norse settlers, who were not enthusiastic taxpayers or tithers, may have retreated to the inland valleys at the sight of the taxman, taking with them as many animals as possible. Ivar found no one, but there is some evidence that the settlement did not die out entirely until the closing decades of the fourteenth century: one human bone found in the Sandnes graveyard has a radiocarbon range of 1390–1428. All other samples have an earlier radiocarbon range. It would be imprudent to build an argument on the analysis of a single bone, but it is at least possible that a few Norse lived in the Western Settlement until 1400. The excavation of 'The Farm beneath the Sand' (Danish: Gården under Sandet, so known in the archaeological literature as GUS) in the 1990s implied late occupation, and the subsequent analysis of soil, using accelerator mass spectrometry dating, suggests that the farm was occupied until c. 1400. In short, Ivar was wrong.

If, on the other hand, Ivar's real purpose was, as he says, to expel the skrælings who had attacked the settlers, one might expect that the graveyards would yield evidence of violent deaths; that has not been the case. And if the Thule had slaughtered the settlers, why had they not slaughtered the domestic animals for food? The paucity of personal items in the ruins of the Norse farmsteads, and of bell metal fragments in the ruins of the churches, implies a planned exodus, not a hurried flight. But where did the settlers go? This gap in the documentary record has been filled by those who want the Norse Greenlanders to have settled on the North American mainland.

The principal evidence adduced by such enthusiasts is an entry in the Skáholt Annals (Latin: *Annalium in Islandia Farrago*), which survive in a manuscript in the Bodleian Library in Oxford. The selection of items from the annals is the work of Gísle Oddsson, bishop of Skáholt from 1630 to 1638. The Latin translation of the lost Icelandic original was done by Gísle's colleague Ketill Jörundsson. The relevant entry reads

> Year 1342. The [Norse] Greenlanders freely abandoned the true faith and the Christian religion, and repudiated honest practices and true virtues, and turned to the peoples of America.
>
> [*Anno 1342 Grönlandiæ incolæ a vera fide et religione Christiana sponte sua defecerunt, et repudiatis omnibus honestis moribus atqve veris vertutibus ad Americæ populos se converterunt*]

The phrase *Americæ populos se converterunt* has been taken to mean that the inhabitants of the Western Settlement had decamped to the North American mainland. The difficulty is that *Americæ populos* is a phrase that makes sense in seventeenth-century Latin, but not fourteenth-century Latin. The Norse term that Ketill was translating must have been *skrælingar* (the plural of skræling). In short, the phrase implies assimilation to Thule paganism, not emigration. In Ketill's Latin, however, emigration to the American mainland was implied, and that started a hare that was then pursued by those determined to show that the Norse settled on the mainland well before Columbus sailed. There were in due course reports of sightings of people (including bearded men) that in the early twentieth century were described as 'blond Eskimos'. Genetic research published in 2003 demonstrated that there was no overlap in the DNA of the Copper Inuit (as the 'blond Eskimos' are now known) and the people of Iceland. Such science is of course dismissed by true believers. It is simply not known where the people of the Western Settlement went: they may have moved to the Eastern Settlement, or to Iceland, or to mainland Scandinavia.

The end of the Eastern Settlement, and therefore of the Norse presence in Greenland, is similarly undocumented. Nothing in writing attests to the survival of the settlement beyond the first decade of the fifteenth century. There are indications, however, that the settlement lasted until at least middle of the century. The latest human remains are those at Sillisit Church (near Qassiarsuk), which have been dated to c. 1450. The most revealing evidence, however, is the extraordinary cache of clothing excavated from the churchyard at Ikigaat (Norse: Herjolfsnes) in 1921, and expertly re-examined by Else Østergård at the turn of the twenty-first century. The Norse residents of Herjolfsnes did not use precious driftwood to build coffins, but rather buried their dead in layers of clothing that had been made in Greenland. Most of the clothing styles had only been known from European paintings, but the Herjolfsnes excavations yielded twenty-three complete costumes (including three children's costumes), sixteen hoods, four caps, and five stockings. There was much more medieval clothing in this cache than survives in all of Europe. Radiocarbon dating suggests c. 1434 for the newest garment.

Much scholarly attention has focussed on one find: a tall brimless hat (worn with a hood) known as the 'Burgundian cap', which came to symbolize the European connections of the Norse Greenlanders in the final years of the settlement. Poul Nørlund, who was the principal excavator in 1921, noted a resemblance to Burgundian hats familiar from Flemish paintings and statues, and concluded that it represented a late fifteenth-century Burgundian style. This happy picture was shattered in 1996, when Jette Arneborg, the doyenne of Norse Greenlandic studies, announced on the basis of radiocarbon analysis that the cap was made at least a century earlier than Nørlund's date (1250–1410), and argued that its style conformed to Nordic rather than Burgundian styles. The most recent analysis, in 2014, shows that separate parts of the hat were considerably older than the sample tested by Dr Arneborg, and pushed the date back to the thirteenth century. In short, the cap has nothing to do with the end of the Greenland settlements.

Two fifteenth-century papal letters shed refracted light on the increasingly vague knowledge of the surviving Greenland settlement. An apostolic letter of 20 September 1448, written in the name of Pope Nicholas V, declares that Greenlanders had been true to the Christian faith for almost six centuries, whereupon thirty years previously (i.e. c. 1418) there had been an attack:

Thirty years ago a fleet of barbaric pagans arrived by sea from neighbouring coasts to invade the country and cruelly attacked the inhabitants, destroying their native land and its sacred buildings by fire and sword until there was nothing left on this large island except for nine parish churches that could not be reached by the invaders because of the height of the mountains. The unfortunate natives, both men and women, particularly those strong enough to bear the yoke of slavery, were enslaved in their own region, as if they were the subjects of a tyrant. The same report says that the captives later returned to their native land, and rebuilt their homes and churches

[*ex finitimis littoribos paganorum ante annos triginta classe nauali barbarj insurgentes cunctum habitatorum ibidem populum crudeli invasioe aggressi et ipsam patriam edesque sacras igne et gladio deuastantes solis insula nouem relictis ecclesijs parrochialibus que latissimis dicitur extendj terminis quas propter crepidines montium commode adire non poterant miserandos utri- usque sexus jndigenas illos precipue quos ad subeundum perpetue onera seruitutis aptos uidebant et fortes tanquam ipsorum tyrannidj accommodatos ad propria vexerunt captiuos verum quia sicut eadem querela subiangebat post temporis successum quam plurimi ex captiuitate predicta redeuntes ad propria et refectis hinc inde locorum ruinis diuinum cultum possetenus ad instar dispositionis pristine ampliare et instaurare*]

The report on which this account is based has not survived.

This letter presents many difficulties. Greenland had not been Christian for 600 years, nor are any of the known parish churches inaccessible or close to the mountains (they are mostly close to the shore). Some houses show signs of house fires, but there is no evidence of large-scale destruction. The letter may reflect a distant memory of a raid, but even the identity of the raiders is not clear. The Thule are obvious candidates, but there is no evidence that they had either the numbers or the weaponry required to overwhelm the Norse. 'Fire and sword' is a common collocation (Livy has *omnia ferro ignique vastata*—'everything was destroyed by fire and sword'), but it seems an odd phrase to use about a people who had no swords. The raiders could have been English, who had both swords and a record of brutality in the North Atlantic, but there was no treasure to be looted in Greenland and no motive for attacking people with whom they traded. And the English were not regarded by the Church as pagans.

The most likely explanation is that Chancery (or the papal secretary who wrote the letter) had been badly briefed by someone who had a motive to do so. The letter was addressed to the bishops of Hólar and Skálholt. The bishop of Skálholt was Marcellus de Niveriis, a criminally corrupt German Franciscan friar who never went to Iceland, but was happy to take the income from the see. Bishop Marcellus was in Rome when the apostolic letter was written, and it is possible that his plans for personal profit included selling the bishopric of Gardar on to the highest bidder, perhaps working with his colleague in Hólar. In short, the letter is worthless as a tool for understanding the end of the Greenland colony.

On 9 July 1492 Cardinal Rodrigo Borgia nominated the Benedictine Mathis Knutsson as bishop of Gardar. It was the last of his many nominations to benefices, because a month later (11 August), Cardinal Rodrigo was elected as Pope Alexander VI. He then wrote to the bishops of Hólar and Skálholt ratifying his own nomination. The letter begins with a statement of the Pope's understanding of the state of the church in Greenland. This account would have been informed by contemporary knowledge in Norway, as Cardinal Rodrigo's practice was to sponsor nominations by secular powers, in this case those of the kingdoms of the Kalmar Union.

> We have been informed that in the diocese of Gardar in Greenland, which is situated at the edge of the known world, that the people, because of the shortage of bread, wine, and oil, live mostly on dried fish and dairy products. Because of the difficulties of navigating through the huge amount of sea ice, and because of the infertility of the land and the difficulty of living there, ships rarely land there.

Indeed, we have learned no ship has called there for eighty years, because Gardar is icebound except in August, and therefore there has been no resident bishop or priest for eighty years. Many Catholics have therefore forsaken the faith into which they were baptized. There is said to be no memory of the Christian faith except for an altar cloth which is shown to the people once a year. This cloth is the corporal on which the last priest consecrated the body of Christ a century ago

[*Cum ut accepimus ecclesia Gadensis in fine mundi sita in terra Gronlandie, in qua homines commorantes ob defectum panis, vini et olei, siccis piscibus et lacti uti consueuerunt; et ob id ac propter rarissimas navigationes, ad dictam terram causantibus intentissimis aquarum congelationibus fieri solitas, navis aliqua ab octuaginta annis non creditor applicuisse; et si navigationes huiusmodi fieri contingeret, profecto has non nisi mense Augusti congelationibus ipsis resolutis fieri posse non existimentur; et propterea eidem ecclesie similiter ab octuaginta annis vel circa nullus penitus episcoporum vel presbyterorum apud illam personaliter residendo prefuisse dicitur. Unde ac propter presbyterorum catholicorum absentiam evenit quamplurimos diocesanos olim catholicos sacrum per eos baptisma susceptum (proh dolor) renegasse, et quod incole eiusdem terre in memoriam christiane religionis non habent nisi quoddam corporale, quod semel in anno presentetur, super quo ante centrum annos ab ultimo sacerdote tunc ibidem existente corpus Christi fuit consecratum.*]

The reported lack of bread, wine, and oil is not merely a regret that the essentials of a Mediterranean diet were not available in Greenland. All had a sacramental significance: bread and wine in the Eucharist, oil in baptism and the anointing of the sick. Such lacks were therefore an impediment to the practice of the faith.

Eighty years before 1492 is 1410, which happens to be the date of the last ship known to have sailed for Greenland from Norway. It is not clear how the touching story of the corporal was transmitted to Rome, nor is the practical question of how the new bishop would reach Gardar. In the event, the journey was not necessary, and Mathis became yet another bishop who did not go to Greenland. Again, the letter casts no light on the date or causes of the abandonment of the settlement.

There is evidence that European ships continued to visit Greenlandic waters until the end of the fifteenth century, but their purpose was fishing rather than trade, so there was little occasion for contact with any remnant of the Eastern Settlement. Most of these ships were English, sailing from Bristol, but Hanse ships were fishing in the same waters. The settlement disappeared sometime in the fifteenth century without anyone noticing. Inevitably, a story arose about the last Norse Greenlander, in this case recorded in the 1620s by an Icelander called Björn Jónsson, from Skarðsá. Björn's annals recount the tale of Jón the Greenlander, so called because he had been on three ships that had drifted to Greenland. In about 1540 Jón is said to have been on board a Hanse ship from Hamburg when it drifted into a fjord, and the sailors saw on an island an abandoned settlement with houses, boathouses, and fish racks similar to those in Iceland. They found the body of a man lying face down. He was wearing a cloth hood and clothes of wool and sealskin. Beside him a lay a knife, which Jón took with him. The legend of the last Norse Greenlander was born.

The question of why the settlements died out has long been a subject of debate. The seven dominant arguments are failure to adapt, climate change, ecological depletion, the ivory trade, ethnic conflict, assimilation, and emigration.

The best known of these theories, thanks to Jared Diamond's best-selling *Collapse: how societies choose to fail or succeed* (2005), is the contention that the Norse failed to adapt to local conditions and that the Eastern Settlement suffered a sudden collapse. Diamond is intelligently alert to a variety of factors, but his argument that the Norse (in contrast to the Thule) had failed to adapt to local conditions, instead insisting on living like Europeans, is problematical. The Norse lived in Greenland successfully for centuries, and they certainly adapted their diet and their architecture as conditions changed. Diamond also doubted that the Norse hunted walrus, and (very oddly) insisted that they had an irrational prohibition against eating fish. Greenland specialists have offered nuanced rebuttals of the collapse hypothesis (see Berglund, 2009, and Dugmore, 2012, in Further Reading), but specialist academic studies have little appeal to mass audiences.

Diamond's central contention is that the Eastern Settlement collapsed suddenly. He compares the last days of the settlement to

> an overcrowded lifeboat...famine and disease would have caused a breakdown of respect for authority...starving people would have poured into Gardar, and the outnumbered chiefs and church officials could no longer prevent them from slaughtering the last cattle and sheep...I picture the scene as...like that in my home city of Los Angeles in 1992, at the time of the so-called Rodney King riots...thousands of outraged people from poor neighbourhoods... spread out to loot businesses and rich neighbourhoods

This is fantasy history. There is no evidence that the abandonment of the settlement was anything but orderly.

The second theory centres on climate change. Contemporary science demonstrates to anyone open to arguments from evidence that (in the authoritative words of the Royal Society) 'recent climate change is largely caused by human activities.' Reconstruction of the climate of the past, however, is more problematical, because of a shortage of reliable data and an evidence base that is fragmentary. There is evidence from ice core samples and historical documents for a period of warmth in the early medieval period, variously called the 'medieval warm period', the 'medieval climate optimum', or the 'little climate optimum'. According to this hypothesis, from the mid ninth to the mid thirteenth centuries, Greenland's glaciers were in retreat and trees were able to grow on sites where they could not grow in the centuries that followed. A study based on ice cores in Greenland placed the maximum warming at 975 CE, when Iceland and Greenland were relatively free of ice and the Greenland settlements were beginning. A study based on documents concluded that the mildest period in Greenland occurred in the late eleventh and early twelfth centuries. Ice core samples from northern Greenland imply a cold wave beginning in the late twelfth century. The Norse would therefore seem to have settled in Greenland in a period when the climate was warming and the ice was retreating.

The notion of a Little Ice Age in the northern hemisphere from the late twelfth to the late nineteenth century commands widespread acceptance, though it is acknowledged there were intermittent clement periods. During this period of cooling, which may have been accelerated by the massive eruption of Mount Samalas, on Lombok (Indonesia) in 1257, glaciers advanced, sometimes across upland pastures, and sea ice increased. Another fluctuation became evident in the warming that began early in the twentieth century, this time exacerbated by anthropogenic warming in the wake of the coal fires of the industrial revolution.

Greenland was a satisfactory place for pastoral farming when the Norse arrived, as indeed it is now. From the twelfth century to the fifteenth, however, pastoral farming became increasingly challenging as summer pastures shrank and growing seasons became shorter. For subsistence farmers, the consequence of diminished harvests was a shortage of fodder for the winter season, and animals that could not survive on meagre rations had to be slaughtered. During the same period summer sea ice gradually increased, blocking the normal route to and from Iceland, making navigation within the settlements more difficult, and rendering harbour seals more inaccessible to hunters.

The third theory is ecological depletion. This is a model that was long used as an ecological fable to explain the population collapse on Easter Island: the Polynesian inhabitants were said to have destroyed the palm forests in order to secure logs on which to roll the *moai* from the quarries to their gazing positions, and to have hunted the birds to extinction. This model of environmental degradation (which is wholly insufficient in the case of Easter Island) has been applied to various other societies, including Norse Greenland. A layer of charcoal in the soil (described by soil scientists as a 'charcoal-rich horizon') has in the past been taken as evidence that when the Norse arrived, they degraded their environment by burning woodland and other vegetation. Research published in 2013 (see Bishop, 2013, in Further Reading), however, indicates that the charcoal layer was more likely formed by the addition of midden material to infields in the thirteenth and fourteenth centuries. Pollen analysis has shown that flora changed between the tenth and fifteenth centuries, but that change seems to be the result of changing climate rather than human intervention. This is not, of course, to deny that ecological depletion is not a threat. Greenland's whale population was almost wiped out in the nineteenth century, and today, the world's tropical and boreal forests are disappearing at an alarming rate. In the case of Norse Greenland, however, environmental degradation does not appear to have been a significant factor.

The fourth factor concerns the ivory trade. In the early days of the settlements, walrus ivory was a highly profitable export; indeed, the ivory trade may have been one of the principal motives for the original settlements. There was also a market for narwhal tusks. In the thirteenth century, however, elephant ivory from sub-Saharan Africa began to appear on the European market, and in southern Europe was preferred to marine ivory. In Scandinavia, however, walrus ivory continued to be preferred. A lack of data makes it difficult to judge how much this shrinking of the market affected the price that walrus ivory fetched in Greenland. The price did not fall sufficiently for the hunts to be discontinued, but by the mid fourteenth century the volume of Greenlandic ivory being exported had declined. By the end of the century, control of the North Atlantic had passed from Norway to the merchants of the Hansa and their English competitors; both were focussed on the market for fish rather than luxury goods, and so had little reason to call on the Norse settlements in Greenland. This shift may well have been a factor in the decline of the Greenland settlements.

The fifth possibility is ethnic conflict. If the sagas are to be believed, the Greenland Norse were willing to murder skrælings without provocation. It is possible that the Thule were similarly violent: an entry in the Icelandic Annals for 1379 records, with an unknowable degree of accuracy, that skrælings attacked the Norse Greenlanders, killing eighteen men and enslaving two boys. The Norse had been abandoned by the state, and the Thule had never formed one; such an environment leaves ample room for ethnic feuds. There was competition for game on hunting grounds, and the Thule may have regarded grazing domestic animals as legitimate booty. Norse goods have been found in Thule sites, and Thule goods in Norse sites, but there is no evidence to show whether such exchanges were peaceful: the objects could have been traded or looted. In short, it is impossible to tell whether ethnic violence was a factor in the final years of the Eastern Settlement. A variant on the theme of ethnic conflict is attack by foreign pirates arriving in large ships. Hinrick Rink, a nineteenth-century geologist who worked extensively in Greenland, compiled an extensive collection of Inuit folk tales, in which there is reference to the arrival of foreign ships. This is, like the Norse sagas, difficult evidence to assess, in part because the oral tradition may not transmit stories from the Norse period, but rather the early period of Danish colonization.

Sixthly, the Norse may have been assimilated. Philologists have identified possible Norse loan words in Greenlandic, but the list is short, and it is difficult to be confident that the loans did not enter Greenlandic after the return of the Danes in the eighteenth century. Recently it has become clear that there is no genetic evidence to link the Inuit to the Norse or Celtic (or Dorset) population in medieval Greenland (see Molte, 2014, in Further Reading). In short, there is no longer a case for assimilation.

Seventhly, the Norse may simply have slipped quietly away, possibly to Iceland, but more likely to Norway. The Black Death struck Norway in 1349, apparently carried to Bergen in a ship from England laden with grain and infected rats. In the next six months almost half of Norway's population died. Land was left bereft of tenants. Empty farmland in Norway would have been an attractive prospect for a Greenland farmer straining to survive on increasingly marginal land. And if the final departure was preceded by a gradual diminution of population from a high point of c. 2,000–3,000 to fewer than 1,000, the remnant would be vulnerable to a catastrophe that robbed the settlement of its labour force. Scholars have rightly suggested that such a calamitous event would likely take the form of a loss at sea. A helpful analogy might be the Eyemouth disaster of 1881. Eyemouth is a fishing village on the east coast of Scotland, a few miles north of the English border. On 14 October the village fishing fleet, together with some boats from neighbouring villages, was caught in a storm. Of the forty-five boats that went to sea that day, only twenty-six returned. In a single day 189 men had perished, 129 of them from Eyemouth village. The community did not recover for decades. Such an event could have overwhelmed the last members of the Norse community in Greenland. We simply cannot know.

My principled uncertainty is not shared by those with strong convictions. The most strident voices are those who believe that the Norse Greenlanders moved west to the North American mainland. This theory, which quickly became a certainty, first arose in antebellum America. The Norse Greenlanders had left to join the Christian colony in Vinland, in what is now the United States, and after several centuries that colony had disappeared. The mystery of disappearance was not in Greenland, but in America.

The limits of the Norse presence on the North American continent will be the subject of chapter 7, but first we must turn to the only known North American Norse site beyond Greenland, a staging post to Vinland.

CHAPTER 6

L'ANSE AUX MEADOWS

The first person to suggest that Newfoundland might have been a stopping point on the journeys that took Europeans to America was Benjamin Franklin, who in a letter of 1781, commenting on the possibility that an inscription found near Taunton (Massachusetts) might be Phoenician, wrote,

> If any Phenicians arriv'd in America, I should rather think it was not by the Accident of a Storm, but in the Course of their long and adventurous Voyages; and that they coasted from Denmark and Norway, over to Greenland, and down Southward by Newfoundland, Nova Scotia, &c., to New England; as the Danes themselves certainly did some ages before Columbus.

These lines, written long before Americans could read the sagas, now feel prophetic. The truth of the contention that 'Danes' had coasted 'Southward by Newfoundland' would not confirmed for another two centuries.

In 1905 a Newfoundlander called W. A. Munn published a pamphlet entitled *Wineland Voyages, Location of Helluland, Markland, and Vinland*, in which he argued that Norse seafarers led by Leif Eirikson must have made landfall near L'Anse aux Meadows, a fishing village at the northernmost tip of Newfoundland's Great Northern Peninsula. He suspected that settlement was established either at Pistolet Bay, or (less likely) Sacred Bay. In the late 1930s, a

Finnish geographer called Väinö Tanner searched Épaves Bay, on the eastern side of Sacred Bay, but, like Munn, was unable to find evidence of a settlement. Tanner believed that the Northern Peninsula was Vinland. He was also the originator of the (incorrect) theory that the *vin* (with a short i) in the sagas meant 'pasture' or 'meadow', whereas *vín* (with an acute accent indicating a long i) meant 'wine'; he therefore proposed to look for meadows rather than vines. In the early 1950s the search was resumed by Arlington Mallery (author of a book on the pre-Columbian iron age in America), who walked the shores of Pistolet Bay, but to no avail. In 1959 a reputable Danish archaeologist called Jørgen Meldgaard had conducted a rigorous search of Pistolet Bay, but found nothing of significance.

Finally, in 1960, a Norwegian explorer called Helge Ingstad arrived in Newfoundland in search of Vinland. He began by sailing along the east coast, stopping at 'outports' (coastal villages) to enquire about traces of old settlements. His enquiries were sometimes greeted with suspicion, as he was assumed to be hunting for buried treasure. Nothing of promise came of his enquiries, so, pursuing the suggestions advanced by Munn, Ingstad then sailed to the northern tip of Newfoundland's Great Northern Peninsula. He inspected Pistolet Bay, and then moved on to L'Anse aux Meadows, the name of which reminded him of Väinö Tanner's view that 'vin' meant 'meadows'. On landing, he met a man called George Decker, who explained that there were indeed earthworks at a place called Black Duck Brook, which emptied into Épaves Bay. They walked together to Black Duck Brook, where Ingstad saw overgrown earthworks that looked like the site of houses (Fig. 6.1). Ingstad decided to excavate the site. Fortunately, his wife Anne Stine was an archaeologist who had trained at University of

Fig. 6.1 Earthworks, L'Anse aux Meadows

Oslo, and she knew how to excavate. In the years 1961 to 1968, Helge organized and Anne Stine directed seven seasons (i.e. summers) of excavation, with archaeologists from five countries (Canada, Iceland, Norway, Sweden, and the United States) participating. They excavated eight building sites: three halls (each with several rooms), three huts, a small house, and a hut with a smelter for making and working iron. The buildings were made of turf mounted over wooden frames (like Icelandic houses), and seem never to have been altered, which implies a relatively short period of occupation. That might help to explain why there is no burial site.

There is also no evidence of farming: there are no animal pens or shelters, and the pollen record yields no evidence of grazing. This puzzled the Ingstads, as the sagas concur in the assertion that Thorfinn Karlsefni brought cows and a bull to Vinland. They noted, however, that the *Saga of Eirik the Red* adds what may be a

Fig. 6.2 Spindle whorl, L'Anse aux Meadows

pertinent detail, which is that the cattle were kept on an island (thus obviating the need for fences). Green Island, just off the coast of L'Anse aux Meadows, certainly offers the requisite grazing.

The excavations led by the Ingstads yielded artefacts that placed the identification of the site as Norse beyond reasonable doubt. One was a spindle whorl, found in 1964 (Fig. 6.2). The gendering of tasks in Norse society means that the soapstone spindle whorl, which had been used as the flywheel of a handheld spindle, may constitute evidence that there were women in L'Anse aux Meadows, as may the fragment of a bone needle that is likely to have been used for knitting. In 1968 a second important artefact was unearthed, this time a ringed pin made of bronze, of a type used by Norse men to fasten their cloaks (Fig. 6.3). Other finds included a small whetstone (for sharpening needles), and a large number of iron rivets of a type used in boats. There was also a white glass bead found at the site, but it was lost when it was sent to Ottawa for analysis.

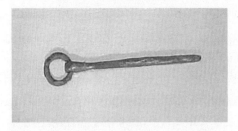

Fig. 6.3 Ringed pin, L'Anse aux Meadows

The most compelling evidence of links to the North American mainland is butternuts (*juglans cinerea*, sometimes called white walnut). Three nuts were found, as was a burl of butternut wood that someone had begun to carve. The butternut has never grown in Newfoundland. Its range includes the St Lawrence River Valley, the Southwest Miramichi River Valley in New Brunswick, and the New England coast, especially where rivers drain into protected coves. Currents would not have brought nuts in the direction of Newfoundland.

The smelter hints at what may have been the most urgent task of those living at L'Anse aux Meadows, which was the repairing of damaged boats. The purpose of the smelter, which was fired by charcoal made in a nearby kiln, was to create iron nails, of which one survives intact. The raw material was bog ore, which was dug out of the brook. There was also a need for carpentry, as boat planks had to be fashioned and fitted; artefacts attesting to this activity include the tip of a bow that powered a carpenter's augur, and a floorboard from a small boat (the towboat for an ocean-going cargo ship known as a *knörr*). Almost 1,500 pieces of worked wood have been recovered from the bog, and tool marks bear mute witness to the metal and stone tools that fashioned them.

The spindle whorl, bone needle, and whetstone hint at textile production and the repair of clothing, sails, and fishnets. The whorl was fashioned from a fragment of a broken cooking pot and was probably used to spin wool that had been carried on the voyage with a view to making *vadmal* (Old Norse *vaðmál*; see Glossary) on a warp-weighted loom; a pile of nineteen stones found in one of the huts may be further evidence of the presence of a loom. The small whetstone and the fragment of a bone needle imply *nålbinding*, a form of single-needle crocheting widely practised in the Norse world for the production of mittens and socks (exemplified by the tenth-century Coppergate Sock in York). The Ingstads concluded that they had found Leifsbudir, Leif Eirikson's settlement in Vinland.

One of the excavators who assisted the Ingstads was Birgitta Linderoth Wallace, a Swedish-Canadian archaeologist who was to remain associated with the site for forty years. The coincidence of a supremely important site being placed in the hands of a supremely gifted archaeologist has been a boon for both public and scholarly understanding of the site. It was Wallace who successfully dislodged the view the Newfoundland was Vinland. She identified L'Anse aux Meadows as a gateway community, the base from which the Norse struck out to the south, where they encountered the grapes and self-sown wheat of the sagas, the butternuts whose shells were excavated in the digs, and the sources of timber that they harvested at Hop. Vinland, the source of all these products, is in Wallace's judgement likely to be the north-east portion of what is now New Brunswick.

Birgitta Wallace also presided over the scientific investigation of the site. This has included radiocarbon analysis, to which 154 artefacts have been subjected; about a third of these are from the period of the Norse occupation. This is a substantial base for analysis, which yields an entirely credible range of dates between 990 and 1050 and a mean date of 1014 CE, which is popularly rounded off at 1000 CE. At the end of the first millennium CE, 500 years before Columbus, there was a Norse settlement in Newfoundland.

What can reasonably be inferred about the settlement? It is likely that it was constructed in the course of a single summer. The solidity of the buildings means that they were intended to be inhabited in all seasons, so the settlement was not a summer camp. It is also clear that the settlement was used as a forward base for the exploration of more hospitable regions. The areas available for sleeping, and the overall scale of the buildings, imply a capacity to accommodate between 60 and 100 people. The buildings are closer together than in Greenland and Iceland (where buildings were on farms), so although the architecture is Icelandic, the population density was much higher than usual. This difference can be accounted for by the fact that the population consisted of ship's crews, not settlers intent on farming. The fact that the settlement in grouped into three suites consisting of a hall and a hut may imply that the settlement was designed to accommodate the crews and passengers of three ships. One piece of evidence that supports this hypothesis is the analysis of jasper firestrikers. In the largest of the three suites, which would have been occupied by the most important group, four of the five firestrikers had been fashioned from jasper from Western Greenland (and the fifth from Iceland); the five firestrikers found in the other two suites came from Iceland.

The social hierarchy probably extended from chieftains to slaves; the latter may have been accommodated in one or more of the huts. There is no evidence of religion at the site, but Iceland became Christian in about 1000 CE, and the known Norse burials in Greenland are all Christian. The first Christians in what is now Canada may well be those who landed at L'Anse aux Meadows.

They seem unlikely, however, to have commended their faith to the Proto-Innu and Beothuk people who were living in Newfoundland. Although the site had been occupied by native peoples at various times, there is no evidence of contact at the L'Anse aux Meadows settlement.

It is also clear that the settlement did not last long. The midden heaps are shallow, there is no church, there is no cemetery, and the buildings were never altered. It seems likely that the site was occupied by the Norse for only a few years, probably less than a decade. The evidence suggests that their departure was orderly, in that nothing of value was left at the site. After the buildings were cleared out, they were burnt, possibly by the departing settlers.

Why was the settlement abandoned? The answer is unknown, but there are various possibilities. There may have been unrecorded conflicts with Proto-Innu and Beothuk people. Another factor may have been distance: the voyage from Brattahlid to L'Anse aux Meadows took longer than the voyage to Norway, and the Labrador coast was largely unknown. Whether this means that contact with Vinland was lost is less certain. It may be that another gateway community was established at a location still unknown, but it seems unlikely that the small Greenland community had the resources requisite for expansion. The Greenland settlers had used L'Anse aux Meadows as a stepping stone to the resources of Vinland, but thereafter their attention seems to have shifted to Markland (Labrador) and Helluland (Baffin Island). L'Anse aux Meadows may be the sole legacy of Norse penetration to the south, but there may have been a settlement at Hop, wherever that was. Unless another doggedly determined Helge Ingstad emerges, we shall never know.

In 1978 L'Anse aux Meadows was inscribed on UNESCO's World Heritage list, and so declared to be of 'outstanding universal value'. It is said to be 'the first and only known site established by Vikings in North America and the earliest evidence of European settlement in the New World. As such, it is a unique milestone in the history of human migration and discovery'. In one sense, such statements seem insensitive to the views of Greenlanders, whose island is palpably part of North America and whose cultural ties are with the people of the Eastern Arctic. Signage on the site goes further, claiming that 'when the Norse met Aboriginal North Americas in Vinland one thousand years ago, it represented the completion of human migration on Earth. Humankind had encircled the globe'. That encircling was not completed in L'Anse aux Meadows (which here stands for Vinland), but in Greenland.

This reservation is not intended to suggest that L'Anse aux Meadows is unimportant. On the contrary, it seems to have been a staging post en route to a short-lived settlement further south and so extends our knowledge of the southern limits of Norse settlement on the continent. The ultimate prize, from the perspective of Canadians and Americans of northern-European descent, would be the discovery of the settlement or settlements on the mainland.

CHAPTER 7

THE LIMITS OF THE NORSE PRESENCE IN NORTH AMERICA

It is clear that the Greenland Norse reached Newfoundland, where the site at L'Anse aux Meadows offers abundant evidence of a temporary settlement. In this chapter I shall turn to the Norse presence in what is now the eastern Canadian Arctic, and then consider evidence that has been adduced for the contention that the Norse reached Northern Ontario, Nova Scotia, and the coast of Maine.

In the summer of 1977, Deborah and George Sabo were investigating a Thule culture site on the Okivilialuk peninsula on the south coast of Baffin Island (known in Inuktitut as Qikiqtaaluk), in Nunavut. On the stone-paved floor of a semi-subterranean Thule house they found a small wooden figurine (5.4 cm × 2 cm × 1 cm) that is popularly (but inaccurately and unhelpfully) known as the 'Viking Doll' or the 'Bishop of Baffin' (now in the Canadian Museum of History) (Fig. 7.1). The surrounding artefacts implied a twelfth- or thirteenth-century date. The figurine has no facial features, but the clothing, which consists of a long tunic and a separate hood, has been carefully carved. The front of the tunic is slit from the waist to the hem, and thin incisions mark the border of a cape resting on the shoulders, and also trace two seams (or

Fig. 7.1 Wooden figurine, Canadian Museum of History

rows of decoration) falling from the cape to the waist. On the chest is an incised cross, of which the horizontal element is clear and the vertical element can be discerned under a microscope. The legs give no hint of footgear. The style and workmanship of the figurine is consistent with Inuit carving in the Eastern Arctic in the twelfth and thirteenth centuries, but the clothing is clearly not Inuit. Indeed, it seems to be a representation of European clothing and has marked similarities to examples of male dress excavated at Ikigaat (Norse: Herjolfsnes), in Greenland. The principal difference is that the Herjolfsnes dresses have no slit at the front, but it is possible that the slit represents the gores or insets. The hood on the figurine resembles a style of European hood and capelet worn in the eleventh and twelfth centuries. The cross is a surprising feature. Christianity had arrived in Greenland in about 1010, and in the succeeding centuries such a cross could be worn by any male, but it is possible that the person represented in the figurine was a priest. In short, the Okivilialuk figurine seems likely to be the representation by a Thule resident of Baffin Island of a generic Norse Greenlander who sailed across the Davis and Hudson Straits and landed on the south coast of Baffin Island.

The Inuit were preceded in the Eastern Arctic by the Dorset people, and there is a growing body of evidence, largely in collections held by the Canadian Museum of History, that Norse Greenlanders interacted with the Dorset people in what they called Helluland, which probably denotes northern Labrador and Baffin Island and possibly islands further north, such as Devon Island (Inuktitut: Tatlurutit) and Ellesmere Island (Inuktitut: Umingmak Nuna); the latter, Canada's most northerly island, is only a few miles from Greenland. The Dorset people carved figurative sculpture, and their subjects include people, animals, and spirits. Some of the humans that they represent in their art seem to have European features or clothing: the faces are elongated, and sometimes appear to be bearded; some seem to be wearing headgear. An antler wand found on a Dorset site on Axel Heiberg Island has two contrasting faces (Fig. 7.2). One shows a broad face with a small nose, and the other shows a narrower elongated face with heavy eyebrows and what seems to be a beard. The former is a conventional representation of a Dorset person, and it is distinctly possible that the bearded figure represents a Norse Greenlander.

Beyond sculpture, a variety of what are likely to be Norse artefacts has been found in Dorset settlements. The Dorset people

Fig. 7.2 Carved antler wand, Canadian Museum of History

fashioned their clothing from animal skins, whereas the Norse Greenlanders spun and wove the wool of sheep and goats. Cordage from Dorset sites has been spun from the fur of other animals, including Arctic hare, Arctic fox, and dog. A Baffin Island site has yielded a three-metre length of yarn spun from the fur of Arctic hare. Archaeologists working on Middle Dorset sites on Avayalik

Island, off the northern end of the Labrador Peninsula, have found yarn spun from the fur of both Arctic foxes and dogs. Such artefacts are not easy to interpret. The near-absence of dogs in Dorset culture makes the presence of spun dog hair anomalous. In Norse society, the gendered division of labour meant that women spun and men wove, so the presence of such artefacts could imply that Norse women were at some point present in Baffin Island and Labrador. On the other hand, spinning is a skill that can be learnt, so it is possible (but unlikely) that Dorset people had somehow learnt the skill. The reason that it is unlikely is that the demanding skills required to spin the short slippery fibres of wild animal fur would ordinarily only be developed by people who already knew how to spin the long and microscopically barbed fibres of sheep wool or goat hair.

Most of the artefacts from Dorset sites have been found in northerly settlements, but one has been found on a twelfth-century Richmond Gulf site, on the east side of Hudson Bay. This is a copper pendant (now in the Museum of Natural History in Washington, DC) that has been fashioned from Norse copper. There is no evidence that the Norse were ever in the area, so the pendant would seem to be evidence of a Dorset trade network originating in Labrador or Baffin Island.

Wooden artefacts also present both evidence of contact and challenges for interpretation. The collections of the Canadian Museum of History include a miscellany of wooden fragments fashioned in ways strongly reminiscent of similar artefacts found in Norse sites in Greenland. These include notched tally-sticks, wood with geometrical decoration, and wood that has been worked with European tools, including saws and iron nails, all found on sites on Baffin Island. Sometimes a design seems to have been transmitted for implementation in another medium, so arrowheads carved from wood found on Baffin Island have shapes similar to arrowheads carved from antler on Norse Greenlandic sites. Further afield, a small basket woven from the root of Arctic willow containing a Dorset artefact has been found far to the west, on Bathurst Island (Inuktitut: Tuktuliarvik); baskets of similar design have been found in Norse Greenland.

The dating of these artefacts is problematical. The discrepancy between the radiocarbon dates from Dorset sites in the Eastern Arctic, which centre on the eighth and ninth centuries (before the arrival of the Norse in Greenland) and the design of the material, which in terms of the Norse Greenlanders seems sensibly dated to the thirteenth and fourteenth centuries, raises the possibility, otherwise unattested, of a European presence in the Eastern Arctic in the centuries before the Norse discovery of Greenland. In 1998 the Canadian writer and environmentalist Farley Mowat, whose *Never Cry Wolf* (1963) had made him famous, spun this fragmentary evidence into a book-length argument to the effect that a people whom he calls the Albans travelled from their homes in the north of Scotland and the Northern Isles to Iceland, Greenland, Baffin Island, and Labrador before reaching Newfoundland in the early tenth century. Mowat's book (1998), called *The Alban Quest: The search for a lost tribe* in the United Kingdom and *The Farfarers: Before the Norse* in North America, is engaging and entertaining, but entirely worthless as a historical investigation. Subsequent scholarly investigation of the artefacts has cast doubt on the accuracy of the early radiocarbon dates because of what seems to be a consistent skewing of measurements in samples excavated from permafrost environments. For the present, it seems more sensible to assume that Dorset interactions were with the Norse, and that Farley Mowat's Albans and Farfarers never existed.

The other issue raised by the artefacts that have been recovered from Dorset sites up to the present is that none seems likely to have been an object of trade. On the contrary, they seem to be domestic objects and refuse, apparently left at shore camps close to Dorset settlements. Such material may cautiously be interpreted as indicative of prolonged and extensive encounters between the Norse and the Dorset in the Eastern Arctic. In one instance, it is the absence of objects of trade that implies the presence of the Norse. In 1977–8, Richard Jordan excavated Dorset sites on Avayalik Island and found fifty-four pieces of walrus bone, mostly mandible and cranial fragments. There were no ivory tusks. It seems reasonable to infer that the Norse may have been trading with the Dorset people at this site.

Similar issues arise from Norse material in Thule sites. In the late 1970s Peter Schledermann and Karen McCullough excavated three Thule sites on the east coast of Ellesmere Island. Excavations revealed many Norse artefacts, mostly datable to the late thirteenth century. Finds included chess pieces, chain mail, knife blades, a carpenter's plane, iron ship rivets, woven woollen cloth, and barrel bottoms. The sheer abundance of artefacts, together with the absence of Norse structures, would seem to imply either salvage from a shipwreck or a successful attack on a Norse ship. In either case, the artefacts are evidence that the Norse were sailing in the High Arctic in the late thirteenth century.

Other Thule sites in the High Arctic have yielded Norse artefacts. On Ruin Island, off the north-west coast of Greenland opposite Ellesmere Island, chain mail and woven cloth were found by the

Danish archaeologist Erik Holtved in the 1930s. Carbon dating of the woollen cloth makes it contemporary with the Ellesmere Island cloth. At a Thule site on the west coast of Ellesmere Island, Patricia Sutherland found a piece of bronze that was part of a weighing balance of the type used by Norse traders, and bronze fragments have been found on Thule sites on Bathurst Island, Cornwallis Island, and Devon Island.

Such artefacts indicate that, for purposes of trade, the Norse began to expand into the Eastern Arctic shortly after they settled in Greenland. There are indications that it was the Norse who travelled to what is now Nunavut, rather than the Dorset and Thule who travelled to southern Greenland. There is no conclusive evidence of Norse settlements in Nunavut, but there is a possible Norse shore station at Cape Tanfield, on the south coast of Baffin Island.

The three adjacent sites (Nanook, Tanfield, Morrison) at Cape Tanfield were excavated in the 1960s and 1070s by Moreau Maxwell, whose command of the archaeology of the Eastern Arctic was shaped by his own discipline of anthropology. This perspective sometimes made Maxwell reticent about making archaeological judgements, so when he discovered a turf and stone building on the site, he simply declared it to be difficult to interpret.

In 2000 the investigation of the Cape Tanfield sites was reopened as part of a larger project called the Helluland Archaeology Project, which was exploring sites on Baffin Island and the coast of northern Labrador. The project was led by Patricia Sutherland, the doyenne of Canadian Arctic archaeologists and Canada's leading authority on the Norse in the Arctic. Dr Sutherland undertook an investigation of museum holdings, notably but not exclusively those in her own institution, the Canadian Museum of Civilization. A few of the Baffin Island artefacts that she inspected seemed to be European in origin, in particular two pieces of spun yarn from the site of Nunguvik on northern Baffin Island. In 2001 Dr Sutherland led the first of a series of excavations of the Cape Tanfield sites. Artefacts recovered in the years that followed included whetstones bearing surface traces of smelted metals, pelt fragments from European rats, and a whalebone shovel similar to the turf-cutters used by the Greenland Norse. Dr Sutherland noted that the design of the turf and stone building was similar to structures in Norse Greenland, and that the shaping of the stones seems to reflect the tools and skills associated with European masonry. Dr Sutherland hypothesized that the Cape Tanfield sites might be a Norse shore station, a site where trading may have taken place.

Dr Sutherland published her preliminary findings in academic journals, and in October 2012 made a public announcement of her work to date. Public interest was intense. The banner headline of the *National Geographic* story declared 'Evidence of Viking outpost found in Canada: sharpeners may be smoking guns in quest for New World's second Viking Site'. The public could be confident of the probity of excavations that were to follow, because they were to be led by a distinguished archaeologist. Patricia Sutherland has since been fired, and denied access to the collection that forms the basis of her research. Material that she and her colleagues had collected has been put into storage. Dr Sutherland has enjoyed widespread support from the academic and museum communities, but she still has no access to the collection that she helped to build. It is hard for me to believe that this did not slow the progress of developing academic and public understanding of the interaction between the Norse and the native peoples of the Eastern Arctic.

The reasons for Patricia Sutherland's dismissal are in dispute, but some have seen in it a political dimension. Archaeology is concerned with origins, and the work of archaeologists is sometimes (e.g. in Israel and South Africa) appropriated into political debates about which group should enjoy the legitimacy of first settlement. The Canadian Museum of Civilization, for whom Dr Sutherland worked, had become caught up in the culture wars overflowing from south of the border. In 2013 the Conservative government rebranded the museum as the Canadian Museum of History. The Conservative government's attempt to create a British myth of origin for Canada meant that funding for Arctic history shifted away from the history of the people of the Arctic and instead concentrated on projects such as the Franklin expedition of 1845, a failed attempt to cross the Northwest Passage in which both the expedition's two ships and their crews were lost. The renewed hunt for the ships succeeded when HMS *Erebus* was found in March 2015 and HMS *Terror* in September 2016.

Dr Sutherland's research for the Helluland Project has been restricted, but there is nonetheless some progress. In 2014 she and two collaborators published a paper in *Geoarchaeology* describing a small stone vessel recovered at a Cape Tanfield site. Analysis of traces of bronze in the vessel, together with small glass spherules, showed that the vessel was subject to a high-temperature process. The investigators concluded that the vessel had been used as a crucible, and so, if it was used on-site (as seems likely), constitutes 'the earliest evidence of high-temperature nonferrous metalworking in the New World north of Mesoamerica'.

In 2017–18, the Royal Ontario Museum in Toronto hosted an exhibition called *Vikings*. The core of the exhibition was imported from Sweden, but those artefacts were supplemented with Baffin Island artefacts borrowed from the Canadian Museum of History. The curator of the exhibition (not an Arctic specialist) played down the significance of the Arctic artefacts, doubting, for example, the importance of the crucible, declaring the possibility that the face on the antler is European to be 'subjective', and asserting that L'Anse aux Meadows is 'the only firm archaeological evidence that Canada has a Viking history'. Asked for comment on this perspective, the Museum of Canadian History issued a cool statement to the effect that the work of the Helluland Project 'does not prove conclusively, longer-term contact between European and Indigenous peoples in the Arctic'.

All the artefacts discussed above relate to interaction between the Norse and the Dorset and Thule peoples. Given the areas where the Norse may have been present, however fleetingly, there is also the possibility of contact with one or more First Nations: the Innu of Labrador, the ancestors of the Beothuk and Mi'kmaq in Newfoundland, and the Iroquois of the lower St Lawrence River. The one artefact that offers what may be evidence for contact with one such group is an arrowhead recovered from the Norse cemetery at Sandnes, a large farm (now known as known as Kilaarsarfik) in the Western Settlement of Greenland (Fig. 7.3). The cemetery was in use from the early eleventh century until the Western Settlement was abandoned in the late fourteenth century. The arrowhead, which is now on display at the National Museum of Denmark, is fashioned from Ramah chert from Labrador or a similar outcrop in Greenland. In terms of style, it does not

Fig. 7.3 Sandnes arrowhead, National Museum of Denmark

resemble Norse, Dorset, or Thule arrowheads. It is, however, very much like those of the Point Revenge Culture (also known as 'Labrador Recent Indian Tradition'), an Innu group that lived on the coast of Labrador from c. 1250 to c. 1450 CE and fashioned their arrowheads from Ramah chert.

The arrowhead is evidence of an encounter. It might have been a friendly encounter for purposes of trade, and the arrowhead might have been carried back to Greenland in a Norseman's pocket, perhaps as a souvenir. The fact that it was found in a cemetery suggests another possibility: the precise location of the arrowhead in the southeast corner of the cemetery is not known, but it is surely likely that it travelled to Greenland embedded in the living or dead body of a Norse Greenlander, and that would imply that contact was not altogether friendly.

Fig. 7.4 Official 1939 photograph of Beardmore relics (sword, axehead, rangel (i.e. rattle) [misidentified as shield handle]), Royal Ontario Museum

A visitor to the Royal Ontario Museum ('the ROM') in Toronto in search of Norse artefacts passes through Daniel Libeskind's spectacular deconstructivist frontage and moves upstairs to the Samuel European Armour Gallery. The contents of one display case include a Norse sword and an axe head. The ROM also holds an associated piece of iron which is now understood to be a rattle (Norwegian *rangel*); the purpose of such rattles is unknown, but they may have been part of a trace for a sledge or cart, or they may have a religious purpose, such as fending off evil spirits. The sword was about a metre long, but the blade is broken in half (Fig. 7.4). The axe head has been fashioned from wrought iron, but is missing the hard steel cutting edge, which must either have been broken off or become so corroded that it left no visible trace in the soil. In 1949 the relics were examined by Johannes Brønsted, a distinguished Nordic archaeologist who was then professor of Nordic archaeology at University of Copenhagen and would soon become director of the National Museum of Denmark. Professor

Brønsted concluded on stylistic grounds that the sword was a type made in eastern Norway between the mid ninth and early tenth centuries, and that the axe was slightly later, from the late tenth to the early eleventh centuries. He took the view that the sword and axe may have been an assemblage, and wryly observed that the Norse owner had his own axe, but had inherited his father's sword.

The labelling indicates that the artefacts are from the tenth century, but offer no information about provenance. The ROM's position with respect to the relics has changed over the years. When they were purchased in 1936, they were prominently displayed as a discovery made near Beardmore, a small mining settlement close to Lake Nipigon, to the north of Lake Superior. The label asserted that the find-spot was a burial 'on a portage on the route from Hudson Bay down to Lake Superior'. No doubts were expressed about their authenticity. In the 1990s they went back on display, but this time with no mention of Beardmore or the alleged discovery. They are now simply identified as pieces of tenth-century Norse armour.

The outlines of the Beardmore story have long been known, but the narrative lacked depth until 2018, when Douglas Hunter published a fine archive-based full-length study called *Beardmore: The Viking Hoax that Rewrote History*. The story began with a railwayman and part-time prospector called James Edward Dodd (known as Eddy Dodd), who claimed that he had found the relics while prospecting for gold in May 1931. In Dodd's account, he had been taking samples from an exposed vein of quartz, and at the point at which the vein turned into the ground, a clump of birch trees had grown. He decided to dislodge the birch with dynamite, and on doing so blasted away the roots and about a metre of spoil. On the freshly exposed rock beneath there lay some rusted pieces of iron, which he tossed to one side in order to continue his sampling. They lay where he had cast them until 1933, when he carried them back to his home in Port Arthur.

In 1936 news of the find came to the attention of Charles Trick Currelly, the founding director of the Royal Ontario Museum of Archaeology (one of the predecessor institutions of the ROM), who invited Dodd to bring the relics to the museum. Currelly later described the meeting:

> It was obvious to me that the weapons were a set, that is, that the axe and the sword were of the same date, which I judged to be about A.D. 1000. I asked Mr. Dodd if he had found anything else, as I knew that there should have been another piece. He said yes, that lying over the bar of metal was something like a bowl that was rusted into little fragments. He had just shovelled them out. This bit of evidence was as it should have been, and since no one unacquainted with Viking things would have known of this iron boss that covered the hand on the Viking shield, I felt, therefore, that there was no question that these things had been found as was described.

Currelly bought the relics on behalf of the museum for $500, and then proceeded to check the provenance. He asked Thomas McIlwraith, an anthropologist at the University of Toronto, to visit the find-spot. In September 1937 Dodd led McIlwraith to the location. The site had been disturbed by blasting and trenching, but McIlwraith saw enough to convince him that the story of the discovery was true. A few months later, John Drew Jacob, a local official in the Ontario Fish and Game Department, offered a supporting statement in which he said that he had visited the site soon after the discovery and had seen the rust stain left imprinted in the rock by the sword. The following year, Jacob elaborated his statement, saying that he had seen the relics in Port Arthur, identified them as Norse weapons, and then visited the site. He dated this visit to 1931, but on checking his diary discovered that he had visited the site and seen the rust imprint in June 1930. Dodd then backdated the discovery from 1931 to 1930. Other witnesses came forward, and the date of the discovery continued to oscillate between 1930 and 1931. Dodd changed his story again, and claimed that he had taken the relics home in 1933, not 1930. The more he changed his story, the quicker it deteriorated.

The story took a dramatic turn when a railway brakeman called Eli Ragotte told a newspaper reporter that he had found the relics while helping Eddy Dodd to clear the basement of the house that he had rented. Ragotte subsequently explained that Dodd told him to leave the weaponry where it lay, because it belonged to J. M. Hansen, the house's owner. When contacted, Hansen made a notarized statement to the effect that he had taken possession of the weapons as security on a $25 loan that he had made to one of his employees, a Norwegian migrant called Jens Bloch. Bank records were consulted, and confirmed that there was indeed such a loan, though for $10 more than the amount that Hansen had specified. Bloch was by this time dead, but his widow was consulted, and she explained that the weaponry had come from the collection of Jens's father, Andreas Bloch, who had been a prominent Norwegian illustrator and a collector of armour. His best-known illustrations are in Fridtjof Nansen's books, such as *Paa ski over Grønland* (translated as *The First Crossing of Greenland*).

In Port Arthur, members of the Scandinavian community were lobbying the provincial government to erect a monument to their Viking, and they were displeased by the accounts given by Ragotte and Hansen. Feeling pressure to which they were unaccustomed, Ragotte repudiated his earlier statement, and Hansen attempted to wriggle out of the consequences of his statement by insisting that there must have been two sets of weapons. Hansen examined that weapons in the ROM, and declared that they were similar but not the same as the ones that he had discovered. It is possible that he was telling the truth, because he declared that there were no hooks on the bar that he had found. In fact the ROM's restorers had found hooks flattened against the bar, and prised them open, so Hansen may have been describing the cache as he had found it.

These inconsistencies did not trouble believers in the authenticity of the find. The relics were declared by a newspaper editor called James Watson Curran to be proof of a Norse burial in Ontario. Curran began to lecture widely on the subject, and in 1939 published a book entitled *Here was Vinland: The Great Lakes Region of America*. He contended that Norsemen, probably in the eleventh century, had travelled from Greenland into Hudson Bay, and thence along rivers to Lake Superior. A few miles from the lake, a Norseman had been buried, and these relics were grave goods that had been uncovered by Eddy Dodd. Curran declared that he had investigated the matter thoroughly, and that he was confident that Dodd's account was truthful. Charles Currelly concurred in this judgement, and set out his case in a series of articles. When he retired from the ROM, the label that he had written was replaced by a more cautious one, which nonetheless concluded that the balance of evidence favoured the authenticity of the claim: 'though the matter may never be settled to the complete satisfaction of everyone, our present evidence strongly supports the view that these objects really were unearthed near Lake Nipigon [near Beardmore]'.

In November 1956, unease in the scholarly community about the authenticity of the discovery prompted the ROM to convene a formal enquiry into the matter. The enquiry was to be conducted by Robert Gowe, a journalist on the Toronto *Globe and Mail*, who was given unrestricted access to the museum's files. His findings were to be made public in a series of five articles in the *Globe and Mail*, a procedure designed to demonstrate to the public that the ROM had nothing to hide. The first article was printed on 23 November 1956, and on the day that it appeared Walter Dodd (Eddy Dodd's adoptive son) telephoned the ROM to say that he wished to retract the sworn statement that he had given in 1939 in which he had supported his father's account of the discovery. He subsequently came to the museum, and on 28 November signed a new sworn statement, in which he said that he had travelled with his 'stepfather' to the place where he had been prospecting and watched him deposit on the ground the sword, the axe head and the bar that he had found in the basement of their house, whereupon they returned to Port Arthur. Several months later, Walter explained, his father had returned to the claim, brought back the three objects, and then started telling people that he had found the weapons while blasting. Walter was subsequently forced to sign an affidavit saying that he had witnessed his father's discovery of the weapons. This statement might have concluded the matter, but Eddy Dodd's widow contended that the second affidavit, far from easing a guilty conscience, had in fact been a spiteful way of smearing the name of Eddy Dodd, whom Walter heartily disliked.

Two days after Walter signed his second statement, another witness stepped forward. A retired prospector called Carey Marshman Brooks alleged that Eddy Dodd's story could not be true because it was he (Brooks) who, in his capacity as an employee of Eddy Dodd, had trenched and dynamited the site where Dodd alleged that he had found the weapons. Gowe concluded that Dodd's story had been fabricated, and a full account of his investigation was published in *Maclean's* magazine the following spring. The ROM withdrew the relics from public display, but the academic community was inclined to censure the ROM for displaying the artefacts long after the find had ceased to be credible. The archaeologist and anthropologist Edmund Carpenter, who was working at the University of Toronto, declared that staff at the ROM, including successive directors, had long known that the story of the discovery was fraudulent, and that they also knew the source of the weapons.

Such academic scruples were not welcome in a country that had come to believe in the authenticity of the find, which by this time had begun to appear in textbooks. In 1965 Farley Mowat declared in *Westviking: The Ancient Norse in Greenland and North America* (1965) that the Beardmore relics, considered together with the Kensington Runestone (see chapter 9), demonstrated that there had been a Norse presence in what is now Ontario and the contiguous part of Minnesota. Elaborating this hypothesis, Mowat deemed it likely that the Norse had established a settlement on the shore of Hudson Strait, and then extended their penetration southward through Hudson Bay, James Bay, and thence up the Albany River to Lake Nipigon, from which they could travel on to Lake Superior and thence to Minnesota. Mowat's celebrity gave his hypothesis authority with the reading public, and he capitalized on the selling power of the relics by writing a children's novel called *Curse of the Viking Grave* in which the teenage protagonist bravely defies a curse on a Viking grave from which he recovers a sword.

The power of the narrative, which seemed to confirm that the first Europeans in North America were the Norse, continues to ensure its survival. In 2011 E. J. Lavoie self-published *The Beardmore Relics: A Novel*, a murder mystery in which an archaeologist who is convinced that the Beardmore relics are genuine is found murdered and a colleague at Thunder Bay University launches an investigation that becomes the subject of the novel. The plot leaves the relics far behind, but the title affirms the continuing life of the Beardmore story.

In the late 1890s the notion of a Norse presence in Canada had had a brief flowering in circles associated with the court of the Governor General. Janice Liedl (see Further Reading) has documented balls organized by Lady Aberdeen (consort of the Governor General) in Ottawa (1896) and Montréal (1898), at which guests dressed as 'Vikings and Viqueens', so affirming, as Lady Aberdeen wrote in her diary, the 'Vikings first discovering Canada' This fashion for celebrating a Norse past faded, in part for want of evidence, but was powerfully revived by the Beardmore relics. The Beardmore myth was nurtured by a racialized narrative of Anglo-Saxon hegemony, but sustained, as that narrative began to fade, by the continued presence of the North in the Canadian imagination. This fascination with the North, which became an aspect of Anglo-Canadian identity that distinguished Canadians from Americans, is enshrined in the fifth line of the English version of the national anthem: 'The True North strong and free' (the parallel French line speaks of Canada knowing how to carry the cross—*Il sait porter la croix*). The Beardmore relics provided a narrative in which the European presence in what was to become Canada was initiated in the voyage that began in the Canadian Arctic. J. M. Mancini, who has written shrewdly on this topic, has pointed to the significance of the campaign in the late 1950s by Prime Minster John Diefenbaker to represent the North not only as a 'new frontier', but also as an important component in the 'national consciousness'. This sensibility was hardened as Canada's sovereignty in the Canadian Arctic was challenged by the presence of scientists from several countries and military personnel from the United States. In such circumstances, the Beardmore relics, and their appropriation into a larger narrative by Farley Mowat, helped to anchor the notion that the forefathers of Canada were the Vikings, who were characterized as 'strong and free'.

We may draw five conclusions. First, we can be confident that the discovery of the Beardmore relics was a hoax. Dodd's story was a fabrication, and in any case it is not possible that iron weapons could have been preserved for a millennium in soil that was so wet that it had to be drained before it could be prospected. Second, it is clear that the relics are genuine. Third, it must be acknowledged that the provenance of the relics is unknown: if the story that Bloch brought the relics to Canada in the 1920s is true (which it may be), then that would provide an explanation; if it is not true, then the only alternative would seem to be that the relics originate in an unknown Arctic grave. Fourth, we know that the Beardmore relics provide no support for the contention that there were Norse travellers in what is now Ontario. Fifth, we know that the myth of the Beardmore relics was sustained by broad social forces that relate to Canadian identity.

Yarmouth is a port and town on the south-west shore of Nova Scotia. In 1812 a retired army surgeon, Richard Fletcher, found an inscribed stone on his property at the head of the harbour. The stone was initially moved closer to his house, and its subsequent peregrinations took it to a local hotel, the public library, across the

Fig. 7.5 Inscription on Yarmouth Stone, Yarmouth County Museum

Atlantic to Christiania (now Oslo), to London (where it was kept in storage during World War I), and, after the armistice, back to Yarmouth, where it is now on display at the Yarmouth County Museum. The stone is inscribed with thirteen characters, which have been variously interpreted (Fig. 7.5). In 1884, the markings were declared to be runic and the language Old Norse, which could be transliterated 'harkussen men varu' and translated as 'Harko's son spoke to his men'. Harko was identified with Haki, one of the Scottish slaves despatched by Thorfinn Karlsefni to explore the land that he had discovered. In 1896 a rival theory was proposed, which was that the inscription was in Old Japanese, and could be translated as 'Katurade, the eminent warrior, has died in peace'. In 1934 a second Old Norse transliteration ('laeifr eriuki risr') and translation was proposed: 'Leif to Eric raises [this monument]'. This translation enjoys enduring popularity, probably because Leif and Eirik enjoy a measure of name recognition denied to Haki. In 1974 a self-appointed authority claimed that the script was Mycenaean Greek, and proposed a translation remarkable for its prolixity ('Exalted Throne: The pure Lions of the royal household sent into the sunset to protect, to seize, and to make a hole in the mighty waters at the summit have been sacrificed—the whole corporate body'). Two years later, Barry Fell, a major figure in the world of pre-Columbian theorists of the period, argued that the inscription was written in early Basque and could be translated 'Basque people have subdued this land'.

In 1934 the Yarmouth stone was integrated into the wider picture of pre-Columbian 'discovery' in a short book by the popular historian Thomas H. Raddall and an ex-military collaborator called Charles Hugh Le Palleur Jones. *The Markland Sagas: With a discussion of their relation to Nova Scotia* argued that the stone was an important constituent of a body of evidence that demonstrated that the Norse in Nova Scotia were the earliest white settlers in North America. They even claimed that the Norse had arrived in Nova Scotia before the Mi'kmaq, thus creating (spurious) justification for the dispossession of the Indigenous people. The Norse were hailed as 'our blood kinsmen', a conflation of Britons and Norse to which I shall return in my final chapter. The difficulty was that the imagined Norse colony in Nova Scotia was short-lived, which raised the awkward question of why 'the courageous Norsemen, conquerors of half the known world', should have retreated 'before an ill-armed mob of savages'. The answer is that they returned to Greenland because Eirik the Red had been killed in a riding accident. The racist characterization of indigenous people that characterizes the language of the book was all too typical of the period, and served as support for the notion that white northern Europeans had a right to the possession of Nova Scotia.

In September 2011 the Yarmouth County Museum and Archives mounted an 'International Runic Stone Symposium' with a view to unravelling the mystery of the inscription. No proceedings from the symposium have been published, but the programme gives some sense of what was said. Richard Nielsen (to whom I shall return in chapter 9) declared the writing to be runic, and adduced comparisons to the Gursten Stone in Sweden, the Narsaq Runic Stick in Greenland, and the Ladoga Rune Stick in Russia, which he dated respectively c. 900, c. 1000, and c. 850. As the Narsaq Stick was found on Eirik the Red's Greenland farm, Nielsen thought it possible that the Yarmouth inscription might be related to the voyages described in the sagas. An alternative hypothesis was proposed by the Welsh historian Alan Wilson, who argued that alphabet used in the inscription is Coelbren and the language is Khumric. Mr Wilson acknowledged that his decades of work on the subject have been 'met with nothing but extreme opposition from the academic community'. It seems safe to assume that the symposium did not conclude with a new consensus. The museum does not take a position on the authenticity of the stone, but when I visited in 2019 I was able to walk the 'Leif Ericson Trail', where signage explained that,

> while we cannot be certain that Leif sailed past, or even set foot upon Yarmouth's shores, a mysterious stone with ancient markings, which may or may not be of Norse origin, has only added to the mystery of a possible Yarmouth-Viking connection.

'We cannot be certain' clearly leaves open the possibility that Yarmouth was indeed the place where Leif first landed.

The writer of the inscription has not been identified, but Dr Fletcher is an obvious candidate. The clarity of the inscription was enhanced in the late 1880s by someone wielding a chisel. This may have been the Reverend Gordon Lewis, the Anglican parish priest in Yarmouth who was to serve as inaugural president of the Yarmouth Historical Society and the Yarmouth Leif Erikson

Society. In 1938 Lewis published a pamphlet entitled *The Cruise of the Knorr: An account of early Norse exploration in America*, in which he asserted that

> Leif Erikson and members of his family visited Yarmouth, left the Yarmouth Stone with his name on it, built a village at Tusket and explored the neighbourhood for 12 years

The imagined Norse village at Tusket was deemed to be the centred on Leif's house, and the Norse colony of Vinland was confidently located at the head of tide on the Tusket River, near Yarmouth.

The consequence of Lewis's championing of the stone have been shrewdly analysed in a sprightly book on public history in Nova Scotia by Ian McKay and Robin Bates (see Further Reading). They document how the stone was claimed in Yarmouth: the local hotel's strapline was 'Where the Norsemen first landed', and there were proposals for a 'Viking National Park'. More broadly, they show how the local claims broadened into the contention that the Norse were the 'essential' Canadians. Such ideas underlie the notion that the Norse settlers were the prototype of today's Canadian citizens. This is an ideology of race. In the words of *Historic Nova Scotia* (1948), 'the Norse discoveries are the first recorded contacts of our race with this continent' and so should be of interest to all members of this race. This exclusion of Indigenous people, Afro-Nova Scotians (the oldest black settlements in Canada), southern Europeans, Jews, and a host of other groups settled in Nova Scotia from the status of 'essential' Canadians is a reminder that the imagined Norse presence in North America has been used to support repugnant ideologies of race.

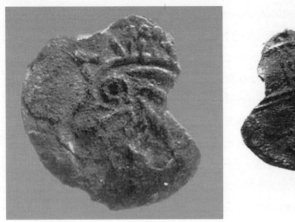

Fig. 7.6 Maine penny

There is one Norse artefact in what is now the United States. In the summer of 1957, an amateur archaeologist called Guy Mellgren was conducting his second season of excavations at Naskeag, an ancient Native American settlement on Blue Hill Bay on the coast of Maine. The land was owned by a man called Goddard, and so is referenced in the archaeological literature as the Goddard site. On 18 August, Mellgren found an old silver coin some 12 cm below the surface (Fig. 7.6). He showed the coin to a local coin collector called Charles Nettleship, who noted the voided short cross (i.e. a cross in which the central parts of the limbs have been incised) on the reverse side, and identified the coin as an English short cross penny, which would place it in the period from 1180 to 1247. This judgement was eventually proved to be wrong, but it was not foolish, because some Norse coinage imitated English designs. Mellgren thought that there were three possible explanations for an English coin in Maine: it had been lost in the Middle Ages; it had been dropped in colonial times; it had been brought from Europe and lost at a later date. He thought that the last of these was the most likely.

In 1974 more than 20,000 artefacts from the Goddard site were donated by Guy Mellgren to the Maine State Museum in Augusta. The coin was later noticed by Bert Farmer, a student working on the collection, who in 1978 published an illustrated article entitled 'Were the English the first to discover America?' The readers of this article included a retired military historian called Riley B. Sutherland, who realized that the coin was Norse. In April 1978 Sutherland left to go on holiday in England, and took with him a copy of Farmer's article, which he showed to Peter Seaby, an eminent London coin dealer. Seaby concurred in the view that the coin was Norse, and by the end of the year had printed a photograph on the cover of his magazine, *Seaby's Coin and Medal Bulletin*. Before it appeared, Mellgren had died, still confident that the coin was English.

On 7 February 1979, Kolbjørn Skaare, a numismatist at University of Oslo, examined the coin in Maine and declared it to have been struck in Norway in the period 1065 to 1080, during the reign of King Olaf III (Olav Kyrre). In the account of the announcement in the *Beaver County Times*, Dr Skaare's judgement was welcomed by Bruce Bourque, the chief archaeologist, who said that the coin 'was either carried to Maine by Indians who traded with Viking settlements in the Canadian Maritimes, or the site was actually occupied for a period of time by Vikings'. He added that 'the chances of the coin being a "hoax" or having been "planted"' were almost non-existent because of the extremely rare and valuable nature of the penny, and because its discoverer paid no attention to it since he simply assumed that it was an English coin brought to Maine in colonial times'.

Skaare's judgement was authoritative (and has never been challenged), and it conferred fame on the coin. *National Geographic*,

Time Magazine, and the *New York Times Magazine* all ran stories on it; the BBC filmed it; and Walter Cronkite, the unimpeachable voice of CBS, announced the discovery on the evening television news. In subsequent decades the importance of the coin has often been affirmed, most authoritatively by the Smithsonian. It is now in the Maine State Museum in Augusta, but is not on display, an anomaly inexplicable except in terms of the politics of museums.

The Goddard site at Naskeag Point had been occupied by Native Americans from c. 1180 to c. 1235, which fell within the circulation period of the coin and within the period of the Norse settlements in Greenland. The presence of a Norse coin on American soil might be deemed to imply that the Norse Greenlanders had travelled as far south as New England, or, at the least, that there were trade links with the Norse in this area. Certainly other artefacts had come from northern regions of the continent, including hundreds of flakes of the translucent stone known as Ramah chert (which could only have been secured from outcrops in northern Labrador or Greenland), a Dorset-culture burin, and what may be a Dorset-culture jade knife. There is also, as I explained earlier, a Point Revenge arrowhead that is similar to the arrowhead found in the Sandnes graveyard. The Goddard coin was pierced near the edge, so it is distinctly possible that it had been worn as a pendant by one of the residents of the Goddard site. That said, parts of the coin have deteriorated, and the piercing is no longer visible, though it is readily apparent in early photographs.

News of the Goddard coin spread beyond the borders of Maine, and it soon came to be known as the Maine penny. It is widely recognized as the only pre-Columbian Nordic artefact in what is now the United States that can confidently said to be genuine. But how did it get there? There are possible explanations other than those adduced by Mellgren. The most radical possibility was proposed by the Edmund Carpenter (who had established his reputation as an exposer of hoaxes with the Beardmore relics) in a pamphlet called *Norse Penny* (2003). Carpenter began by observing that in 1956, the year before the Maine penny was discovered, Hjalmar Holand, the indefatigable champion of the Kensington Runestone (see chapter 9), published *Explorations in America Before Columbus*, in which he described Thorvald Eirikson (brother of Leif Eirikson) sailing along the coast of Maine, and on seeing Mount Desert Island, declaring rapturously that this would be where he would build his home. A year later, a few miles across Blue Hill Bay, Guy Mellgren reported finding a mediaeval European coin. Carpenter wonders if this is a coincidence. Nor was this the only discovery in 1957: this was the year in which the Vinland Map was discovered. It is also the year in which Frederick J. Pohl published his *Vikings on Cape Cod*.

Carpenter observed that no Viking coin has been found in Greenland, and that very few have been found in Iceland or the Faroes; neither Iceland nor the Faroes has yielded an Olav Kyrre coin. This is not, however, a rare coin: in 1879, a hoard of 2,209 Olav Kyrre pennies was found at a farm called Gresli, in Norway. In the course of the next 50 years, the University of Oslo Coin Cabinet, which holds the Gresli hoard, disposed of 942 duplicate pennies from Gresli and other hoards. Of these, 355 went to museums, but the other 587 went to private buyers. In 1948, a New York auction house offered as Lot 663 a collection of 118 medieval Norse coins, 'mostly from the Graeslid hoard'. Lot 663 was bought by the American Numismatic Society for $75—approximately 64 cents each. The ANS no longer has documentation of the purchase, but it does hold 15 Norse pennies, some of which must come from the Gresli hoard. The whereabouts of the other coins is not known, and it seems reasonable to infer that they were subsequently sold or traded.

The implication of this argument is that Mellgren or a contemporary could have acquired the penny. The account of the discovery could be a prank executed by Mellgren, or someone else could have left the coin for Mellgren to find. The counterargument is that Mellgren always thought that the coin was English, and thought that the most likely explanation was that it had been accidentally dropped in relatively recent times. He never claimed that the coin had any particular significance. Carpenter invokes the three verdicts available to courts and juries in Scottish criminal procedure—guilty, not proven, not guilty—and chooses the intermediate verdict of not proven. The two Maine archaeologists who speak with the greatest authority on the coin, Bruce Bourque and Steven Cox, both take a more generous view, and assume that the find was genuine.

In recent years, two investigations have provided evidence that tips the balance further in favour of the find being genuine. First, the coin has been examined by means of the technique known as Raman spectroscopy. The results (which have not yet been published) show that the corrosion on the coin supports the hypothesis that it had been buried in a horizontal position for centuries. Second, the academic numismatist Svein Gullbeck has undertaken a scrupulous study (published in 2017) of the Maine penny in the context of the Gresli hoard. The Maine penny is part of a distinctive subset known as 'Class N' coins, which are characterized by a particular orientation of the head design. The duplicates from the Gresli hoard that were sold included forty-one coins (from a total of 104 coins) of the Class N type, but none was fashioned from the same dies as the Maine penny, so there is no duplicate in the part of the hoard that was retained. It is therefore a unique variant, and all such coins were retained, so it cannot have come from the Gresli hoard. Indeed, it cannot be numbered amongst the 952 coins sold or donated to museums by the University of Oslo between 1881 and 1924. If to that conclusion we add the observation that the Maine penny is in poor condition compared to other coins in the Gresli hoard and in other known hoards, it becomes reasonable to conclude that the Maine penny was a genuine find, and that it constitutes evidence of a trade network that extended as far south as what is now Maine.

But how should the Maine penny be interpreted? When it was displayed at the Smithsonian's splendid *Vikings* exhibition at the National Museum of Natural History in Washington in 2000, the expert opinion of Steven Cox was set out in the catalogue:

> It is unlikely that a Dorset Eskimo could have kayaked down to the end of Naskeag Point, and so these artifacts [the Dorset-culture burin and knife] were almost certainly obtained though Indian trade channels that must have extended north to Newfoundland and Labrador, where Dorset people lived side-by-side with Indians. We suspect that the Norse coin…arrived at the site in a similar manner. There are no other Norse artifacts from the site, and no evidence of a Norse settlement here or anywhere else south of northern Newfoundland.

Dr Cox goes on to concede that the Norse could have visited the site, which would be an obvious place for trade, and notes that new evidence may yet emerge, but sensibly declines to extend his argument further than the evidence. Such scholarly inhibitions do not trouble those who are convinced that there were Norse settlements in America.

CHAPTER 8

AMERICAN RUNESTONES

In some circles, the presence of the Norse in medieval America is understood as a fact. Evidence, in the form of runestones, arte-facts, and earthworks, has been found all over America since the 1830s, mostly in areas of Scandinavian settlement and often by people of Scandinavian descent. The earliest area in which evidence was found was New England, and the first prominent advocate of New England settlement was Rasmus Anderson, the first head of Scandinavian Studies at University of Wisconsin–Madison. Anderson's *America not discovered by Columbus*, first published in 1874, was responsible for popularizing the idea that the Norse were the first Europeans to reach America, and that they subsequently visited America for centuries. The Vinland of the sagas, he declared, was centred on Narragansett Bay, in what is now Rhode Island and Massachusetts. The artefacts at the heart of his argument were the runic inscription on Dighton Rock (in Massachusetts) and the Newport Tower (in Rhode Island).

Dighton Rock is a 40-ton boulder which originally lay in the riverbed of the Taunton River in Berkley, Massachusetts, c. 25 miles east of Providence. The boulder is notable for the inscriptions carved on a flat surface, which include drawings of people and geometrical shapes, some of which have been interpreted as writing (Fig. 8.1). Unlike the Kensington Runestone (discussed in

Fig. 8.1 Dighton Rock, photographed in 1893

chapter 9), there is no suggestion that the inscriptions might be a hoax, but the debate about its origins has continued for centuries. This debate has generated a vast literature consisting of more than 1,000 books and articles, few of which achieve an acceptable scholarly standard. The full-length recent exception to this torrent of mediocrity and tendentiousness is Douglas Hunter's *The Place of Stone: Dighton Rock and the Erasure of America's Indigenous Past* (2017), which is a powerful account of the history and significance of the many interpretations of the inscriptions.

Dighton Rock was known in the colonial period. In 1680 John Danforth, who was to become a prominent preacher and poet, made a sketch of the inscription (now in the British Library) that omitted the bottom portion, possibly because it was submerged by tidal water as he drew. Danforth identified the petroglyphs as Native American, and argued that they drew on what was apparently a Wampanoag oral tradition of a battle initiated by hostile people who had arrived in a ship that was wrecked on the rocks. Within a few years, Danforth's view was occluded by the argument advanced by Cotton Mather that the writing was Hebrew, and so evidence for his contention that Native Americans were descended from the lost tribes of Israel. Cotton's son, Samuel Mather, took up the theme in his compendious *Attempt to shew that America must be known to the Ancients* (1773). Other theories followed. In the eighteenth century many thought that the inscription was Phoenician, and others argued that it was Japanese or Chinese. In 1789 the newly elected President George Washington was shown a transcription of the engraving in the course of a visit to Harvard College, but politely declined to endorse the notion that it was the work of an ancient civilization, insisting instead that it was the work of Native Americans. In that moment, the good sense of a soldier-president dispelled the fog of spurious scholarship, but it soon closed in again.

In the early twentieth century, E. B. Delabarre, a professor of psychology at Brown University, declared the inscription to be Portuguese, the work of the Azorean Miguel Corte-Real, who left Portugal in 1502 to search for his lost brother and was never seen again. Delabarre interpreted the inscription as Latin: MIGUEL CORTEREAL V DEI HIC DUX IND A D 1511, meaning 'I, Miguel Cortereal, 1511. In this place, by the will of God, I became a chief of the Indians'. This interpretation was taken up by Azorean (and mainland Portuguese) Americans, and in 1952 the Miguel Corte-Real Memorial Society of New York City bought fifty acres of land around the rock in order to create a public park commemorating the Portuguese discovery of New England; they planned to leave the boulder *in situ* and to build a coffer dam around it. The following year the land was expropriated by the State of Massachusetts, and the rock was removed to a museum. The museum, however, has remained in the control of the Azorean community, and in 2011, the 500th anniversary of Corte-Real's landing, the regional government of the Azores joined forces with local Portuguese organizations to mount a celebratory festival.

The Azorean appropriation of Dighton Rock dominates local loyalties, but nationally, other theories abound, most recently the claim of Gavin Menzies in 2002 that the inscription is the work of members of a Chinese fleet that arrived in 1421. The most deeply embedded hypothesis, however, is that the inscriptions are Norse. This identification was first advanced by C. C. Rafn in his *Antiquitates Americanæ* (1837). Rafn and his collaborator Finnur Magnussén understood the inscription to be a mixture of runes and Latin letters, which they translated as 'Thorfins and his 151 companions took possession of this land'. They also found evidence that the rock had been initialled by Eirik the Red and Tyrkir the Southerner, a German slave who had sailed with Leif. The pictographs, in this understanding, represented Gudrid Thorbjarnardottir (Thorfinn Karlsefni's wife) and their son Snorri Thorfinnson, together with the bull whose roars Thorfinn used to frighten off the skrælings at Hop. Rafn was delighted to learn that the term Mount Hope derived from the Wampanoag name Haup, because it constituted evidence that this was indeed the site of the Norse landing. Rafn conflated the sagas to declare that Mount Hope Bay (an arm of Narragansett Bay), downstream from the site of Dighton Rock, was both Hop, where (in the *Saga of Eirik the Red*) Thorfinn Karlsefni had established his settlement, and Leifsbudir, where (in the *Saga of the Greenlanders*) Leif had established his settlement. Rafn also took up the allusion to a 'White Men's Land'

(*Hvítramannaland*) in the *Saga of Eirik the Red*, conflating it with the saga toponym 'Great Ireland' (*Írland hið mikla*), and declared that Irish Christians had once settled 'Florida' (the southern part of the eastern seaboard), thus infusing his narrative with a sinister admixture of racial superiority. The notion of Thorfinn and his companions taking 'possession of this land' is an assertion of Norse priority over other Europeans, and the assertion of an earlier Irish colony in 'White Men's Land' is an assertion of racial entitlement. The characterization of infidel skrælings driving away peaceful Christian settlers embodies a myth of Native American savagery that would be recapitulated in the Kensington Runestone. And just as the Kensington Runestone would evoke the Dakota War, so Rafn's reading of Dighton Rock would evoke Metacom's War, the rising of the Wampanoag and Narragansett nations against the English colonists at Plymouth. Metacom (also known as 'King Philip'), the *sachem* (leader) of the Wampanoag and Narragansett confederation, was killed in the Miery Swamp, near Mount Hope. His severed head was displayed on a pole at Plymouth for twenty-five years, which for some modern readers will raise the question of whether savagery should be associated with Puritan colonists rather than displaced Native Americans. Rafn created a myth whereby a site of revenge against savage Native Americans became Thorfinn Karlsefni's Hop, and Metacom's death a just reprisal for the death of Thorvald Eirikson.

The Norse narrative of Dighton Rock has lived on to the present, in tandem with the Portuguese narrative and a host of competing claims ranging from the Phoenicians to the Africans and the Chinese. What these narratives have in common, as Douglas Hunter has argued at length, is the obliteration of Native American history. There are few petroglyphs in New England, so

Fig. 8.2 Newport Tower, c. 1890

comparative analysis in the region is problematical, but one useful analogy has been proposed by Kenneth Feder, who observes that the stylized face on the right side of Dighton Rock is strikingly similar to the faces on the Bellows Falls Petroglyphs, on the Vermont side of the Connecticut River, which forms the border with New Hampshire. Such helpful analogies are of course dismissed by the proponents of pre-Columbian claimants.

The Newport Tower, a round structure in Newport, Rhode Island, was first identified as Norse by C. C. Rafn in a supplement (1841) to his *Antiquitates Americanae* (Fig. 8.2). Rafn pointed out that rounded arches were a feature of Romanesque architecture, and argued that the structure must have been built before the rise of Gothic architecture (characterized by pointed arches), and therefore no later than the twelfth century. He identified the building as a Norse baptistery. Rafn never visited America, so his confident judgements were based on descriptions and drawings provided by his correspondents.

The first scholar to challenge Rafn's conjecture was J. G. Palfrey, the founding dean of the Harvard Divinity School and a prominent Massachusetts politician. In 1858 Palfrey published the first of the three volumes of his *History of New England during the Stuart dynasty*, in which he argued that the tower was a seventeenth-century windmill built by Benedict Arnold, the governor of Rhode Island (and great-grandfather of his namesake, the traitor to the revolutionary cause). Palfrey found Arnold's will, and noted his reference to a building which described as 'my stone built windmill'. He also proposed that the windmill was modelled on Chesterton Windmill (near Leamington Spa, in Warwickshire), close to Arnold's home in England (Fig. 8.3). Palfrey had assumed that Arnold's Newport farm (Lemmington) was named after Leamington Spa, but it was actually named after the village of Limington, in Somerset. The analogy with Chesterton Windmill, however, is compelling. This windmill was built c. 1632–3, probably to the design of John Stone (son of the architect and master mason Nicholas Stone). There have been suggestions that it was built as a folly or an observatory, but the estate accounts imply that it has functioned as a windmill from the outset.

The notion that the Newport Tower is a Norse church attracted powerful support with the publication in 1942 of *The Newport Tower* by the archaeologist and anthropologist Philip Ainsworth Means, a specialist in the ancient civilizations of Peru. Means argued that the tower could not be a windmill, because it has

Fig. 8.3 Chesterton windmill

fireplaces, and advanced the architectural case for it being a church. He argued that an archaeological investigation would help to resolve the debates about the tower. Means died in 1944, but after the World War II his suggestion was taken up by the

Peabody Museum at Harvard. The report of the first archaeological investigation (1951) documented thousands of artefacts (including pottery shards, iron nails, buttons, buckles, and tobacco pipes), all British and all from the seventeenth century. A boot print under one of columns was made with a seventeenth-century boot.

In 1997 the lime mortar used in the construction of the tower was carbon-dated, and yielded seventeenth-century dates. A subsequent three-season excavation (2006–8) yielded more colonial artefacts. Such evidence does not dent the conviction of true believers. In *The Last Kings of North America* (2012), for example, Robert Johnson and Janey Westin confidently identify the Newport Tower as the Norse church, which they date to 1357. They explain that the first elevated floor contained the altar, and that an ambulatory surrounded the base. The controversy continues on various websites, with most pre-Columbian enthusiasts arguing that the tower is Norse, and a minority favouring the view that it is Scottish, the work of Henry Sinclair. In 2018 new evidence (an aerial photograph from 1939) was adduced for the view that the tower is the round nave of a medieval church built c. 1400 by the Knights Templar. Arnold's windmill is thus appropriated to Scandinavian and Scottish myths of origin, and then incorporated into the fictional world created by Dan Brown.

In 1831 what was identified as a skeleton in armour was discovered at Fall River, between Dighton Rock and the sea. Initial thinking was that it was either the remnant of the sophisticated culture that preceded the arrival of Native Americans, or a member of the crew of a Phoenician ship. C. C. Rafn was sent samples of the brass artefacts found with the skeleton and declared them to be Norse, going on to proclaim that the find-spot on Fall River was in Leifsbudir, the settlement of Leif Eirikson in Vinland. Rasmus Andersen went a step further, introducing the possibility that the skeleton was that of Thorvald Eirikson, who had been buried in Vinland.

The perpetual memory of the Fall River skeleton, which was destroyed in a museum fire in 1843, was ensured by the poet Henry Wadsworth Longfellow, who was an enthusiastic subscriber to the white supremacist strand in nineteenth-century thought. Longfellow inspected the skeleton in 1838, agreed that it was Norse, and wrote 'The Skeleton in Armor', in which he connects the Norse skeleton with the Newport Tower. Once again, a tendentious Eurocentric understanding has obscured the actual significance of the skeleton, which was a mid-seventeenth-century Native American burial.

In the late twentieth century, new finds confirmed (in the judgement of believers) the presence of the Norse in New England. In Maine, the most important Norse artefacts (apart from the Maine penny; see chapter 7) are the three Spirit Pond Runestones, which were found in 1971 at Spirit Pond, which is the name of the Morse River at the point at which it widens in front of a dam before it flows into the sea. The stones were found by Walter Elliott, a local carpenter. The stones are small and can be comfortably held in the hand; they are now in a drawer in the reserve collection of the Maine State Museum in Augusta. One stone has a map of the local area, together with some writing and drawings that seem to represent a cluster of grapes and a sheaf of grain; a second has runic letters inscribed on one side; a third has a lengthy runic inscription (sixteen lines) that extends over both flat surfaces. At a later date, Elliott found a fourth stone, which was not disclosed publicly until 1975. The runes say 'Vin(land)' and '1010'. This inscription clearly refers to the voyage of Thorfinn Karlsefni.

A measured attack by Erik Wahlgren, the scourge of American runestones, inexorably followed. In 1982 he published an article in which he pointed out that the map of the local area is the only known runic map in the history of cartography, to which I would add that the Old Norse language had no word for 'map'. It shows the coastline as it was in the late twentieth century, not as it was a millennium earlier. It includes what seems to be an arrow pointing east, supplemented with a phrase that Wahlgren interprets as 'T(o) Ka(nada) two days' ('Kanada' is the modern Scandinavian spelling of Canada). Commenting on the runes, he notes that two are almost unique—the only other stone on which they appear is the Kensington Runestone. He concludes that the Spirit Pond Runestones are a fraud, possibly a joke.

Such a conclusion by an academic did not dampen the faith of true believers. In the 1990s, Suzanne Carlson attempted a transcription and translation, which revealed an uncertain narrative about a storm at sea in which seventeen sailors had been killed. Of the three proper names, two are gods and one is a mortal called Haakon. The mention of Haakon opened up several new narratives. In 2012, for example, Robert Johnson and Janey Westin's *The Last Kings of North America: Runestone Keys to a Lost Empire* identified Haakon as the youthful Haakon VI of Norway, who wintered at Spirit Pond in 1362 before returning home. The inscriptions are deemed to be the work of his court poet (*skald*), and seem to have been a notebook that would enable Haakon to memorise the poem.

This interpretation of the Spirit Pond Runestones has a rival in the view first expressed in 2014 by Scott Wolter, who argued that the stones are evidence of the Knights Templar fleeing to America in 1307, bringing with them the Holy Grail. On this understanding, the Grail is not the cup from which Jesus drank at the Last Supper (and in which Joseph of Arimathea collected the blood of Jesus during his crucifixion), but rather the descendants of Jesus and his wife Mary Magdalene. Old French 'san greal' (holy grail) is deemed to be a misunderstanding: the 'g' should be brought forward to read 'sang real', holy blood. Others have argued that both meanings are in play, in that Mary Magdalene was deemed to be the vessel that carried the bloodline of Jesus *in utero*. One of the runes, a hooked X, appears not only on the Kensington Runestone and the Spirit Lake Runetones, but also on the Narragansett Runestone (see below) found in 1984. Mr Wolter has written a book (*The Hooked X: Key to the Secret History of North America*, 2009) arguing that traditional scholars have been in denial about the hooked X because they assume that the runestones are the work of the Norse, when in fact they were the work of Cistercian monks travelling with the Knights Templar. Apparently the hooked X is a representation of the inverted V (representing a man), a normal V (representing a woman) and a superscribed v, representing a baby girl. In other words, it is a reference to Jesus, Mary, and their daughter Sarah. Such theories are constructed on the shaky foundation of what are palpably fake runestones.

In Massachusetts, two more stones have been adduced in support of a pre-Columbian Norse presence in New England: the Bourne Stone and Noman's Land Island Runestone. The Bourne Stone is an inscribed boulder that can now be seen in the Jonathan Bourne Historical Center, in Bourne. It has been known locally for at least a century, but came to public attention in 1948, when Olaf Strandwold published his *Norse Runic Inscriptions on American*

Stones, declaring that the runes could be translated 'Jesus amply provides for us here and in heaven'. In 1976, however, Barry Fell announced in *America BC* that the stone was Carthaginian, and that the Punic script could be translated 'A proclamation of annexation. Do not deface. By this Hanno takes possession'. Hanno the Carthaginian was deemed to have visited America in c. 500 BCE. In 2014 the eminent Swedish runologist Henrik Williams cast a learned eye on the stone, and declared that the symbols were not runes. This authoritative judgement has not convinced those who are convinced that the stone is Norse.

Noman's Land Island is an uninhabited island about three miles from Martha's Vineyard. It was used by the US Navy as a practice target for aerial bombing from 1943 to 1996. A combination of the danger posed by unexploded ordnance and the island's present status as a sanctuary for migratory birds means that it has long been closed to the public. The island was once inhabited, but after World War I there was only one resident, named Joshua Crane. In November 1926, at low tide, Crane noticed a large black rock with clearly visible markings (Fig. 8.4). Crane contacted an avocational historian called Edward Gray, who was writing a book about Norse visits to New England. Gray photographed the inscription, and sent his photos to specialists at the University of Oslo, who replied that the inscription read 'Leif Eirikson MI'; the MI was interpreted as a date in roman numerals: 1001. A few rune-stone enthusiasts were allowed to visit the island, but were unable to make a detailed inspection of the stone. In 2017 a 'Noman's Land Rune Stone Recovery Project' was launched in order to bring the stone ashore 'in an attempt to determine its place in American and Norse history'. As I write (2019), the stone has not been moved.

Fig. 8.4 Noman's Land Island Runestone

The final important New England runestone is in Rhode Island. The Narragansett Runestone (also known as Quidnessett Rock) is a huge sandstone slab inscribed with nine runes and a punctuation mark. It was discovered in the mudflats of Narragansett Bay by an unnamed clam-digger (known locally as a quahogger) in 1984. The stone is inscribed with two rows of symbols that are said to be runic. The discovery was reported to the Rhode Island government's Historical Preservation and Heritage Commission, who noted that the contours of the find-spot were changing because of the dramatic erosion of the coastline, and that in an aerial photograph taken in 1939, the rock would have been well behind the shoreline; the rock is not visible in the photograph, and so may have been buried. The rock was stolen in 2012, by which time it was close to the low tide line, so rendering the inscription visible and accessible only for a short period as the tide turned. In April 2013 the Rhode Island Attorney General and the Rhode Island Department of Environmental Management announced the safe return of the stone to state custody, and requested the University of Rhode Island to investigate the origin of the inscriptions.

In 2014 Henrik Williams examined the stone at the University of Rhode Island, and submitted a report in which he observed that the runes were taken from different runic systems (see Glossary), and that two of the runes could not appear together on a genuine inscription. He concluded that the inscription was modern—probably late nineteenth or early twentieth century. Scott Wolter subsequently responded to Professor Williams' report, declaring that

> he seems to be out of his element when dealing with the five mysterious runic inscriptions discovered in North America that include the Hooked X symbol, because they do not fit the standard runic record of Scandinavia. They are the Kensington Rune Stone, discovered in Minnesota in 1898, the three Spirit Pond Rune Stones, discovered together in Maine, in 1971, and the Narragansett Rune Stone first discovered in the early 1940s.

Readers can decide where their sympathies lie. Mine are unequivocally with the authoritative scholarship of Professor Williams.

In October 2015 the stone was placed on public display in the village of Wickford, on the west shore of Narragansett Bay. At the dedication ceremony, it was announced that nine elderly witnesses had signed affidavits attesting that they had seen the stone prior to 1963 (and as early as 1945). The purpose of the affidavits was to discredit the confession of a Providence man that he and his brother had carved the runes in 1964. It seems overwhelmingly likely that the elderly witnesses were telling the truth (why would they not?). The signage beside the stone explains that

> Some believe it is a record of a visit to Narragansett Bay by the Vikings or other Norsemen, or Icelandic explorers/trappers, still others a voyage by the Knights Templar. Some believe it was more likely rendered by immigrants to our area, out of national pride, in the 19ᵗʰ–20ᵗʰ centuries.

Once again, a laudable attempt to be balanced results in equal space being given to bizarre theories, in this case the notion of the Knights Templar in America.

The claim of New England to be the site of the first Norse landings in what is now the United States has been contested, notably in Minnesota (the subject of chapter 9), but also in Oklahoma, where at least ten runestones have been found, more than in any other state in the Union. The best known is the Heavener Runestone, an inscribed boulder in south-east Oklahoma near the border with Arkansas. The date when the inscription was first noticed is uncertain: there is solid evidence from 1923, when an enquiry was sent to the Smithsonian, and local oral tradition that reaches back as far as the 1830s, when a Choctaw hunting party is said to have seen it. Signage explains that 'between 600 and 800 AD prehistoric Oklahoma was visited by Scandinavian explorers'. This date is far earlier than any runestone found in other states. One or more Norse ships are said to have come south from Labrador, rounding the tip of Florida, entering the Mississippi River and then the Arkansas River, and then finally the Poteau River, which would have taken them within three miles of the site of the Heavener Runestone.

The inscription mostly uses the character set of the Older Furthark (see Glossary), which is appropriate to the period 600–800 CE. It is interpreted locally as a claim marker declaring that this is 'Glome's Valley'; others have suggested 'Valley of the Gnomes' or 'Little Valley'. The archaeologist Lyle Tompsen undertook a scholarly study of the runestone in 2007, and concluded that unless new evidence emerges, the stone should be regarded as a modern creation. Henrik Williams inspected the stone in 2015, and came to a similar conclusion. Local support for the authenticity of the stone remains strong. The 55-acre site around the runestone was opened as a state park in 1970, and when budget cuts caused state funding for the park (and six other parks) to be withdrawn in 2011, the city of Heavener assumed responsibility for it. There was an understandable vested interest in doing so, in that the runestone brings visitors to a district in need of tourist income. Income is also raised at an annual Viking and Celtic Folk Festival held at Heavener Runestone Park. In the early 1990s the Carl Albert State College in Poteau changed the name of its baseball teams to the Vikings in honour of the Heavener Runestone.

Other runestones have been found in the vicinity. The stone known as Heavener Runestone Number 2 was discovered in 1954, close to Morris Creek north of Heavener; it is now displayed at the Heavener Runestone site. The inscription consists of one large rune (an 'R'), above which is a small cross. There is also a Heavener Runestone Number 3, which contains the same runes as Heavener 2; they may be the work of the same carver. Both are modern.

Until recently, two more runestones have been displayed in the Robert S. Kerr Museum in nearby Poteau, but with the closure of that museum in 2014, they have been moved to the Leflore County Museum at Hotel Lowrey. The Poteau Stone, found by two boys in 1967 about ten miles from the Heavener Runestone, has an inscription of eight letters; the last two are difficult to interpret, but the first six spell something like *gnoiea*. An alternative understanding is that the inscription means 'magic [or protection] to Goli', and that Goli was the nickname of a Norseman called Glome, hence the link to the Heavener Runestone. In 1969, three boys found a runestone lying beside a woodland path near Shawnee. Its five letters, which seem to have been incised with a modern rotary blade, seem to spell (in the letters of the Older Futhark) a name, perhaps Medok. Elsewhere in Oklahoma, there is a Viking Rock on Turley Hill (near Tulsa) with an inscription sometimes interpreted as a date (2 December 1022). Alas, in the considered view of Dr Tompsen and Professor Williams, all of these runestones are modern in origin.

In short, all American runestones are modern fakes, carved to support a Scandinavian claim to the 'discovery' of America. The best known of these is the Kensington Runestone.

CHAPTER 9

THE KENSINGTON
RUNESTONE

S ome 6,000 runic inscriptions, mostly on stone, survive from
the Middle Ages. The most famous of these, at least by the
measure of Google searches, is neither Sweden's Rök Runestone,
nor Denmark's Jelling Stones, but America's Kensington Runestone,
which has been the subject of hundreds of books and articles. In
the Midwest, it has supplanted Dighton Rock as the most important
artefact from Norse America.

In 1898 a farmer called Olof Ohman was clearing land near the
village of Kensington, in Douglas Country, Minnesota, when he
uncovered a large flat stone entangled in the roots of a poplar tree
(Fig. 9.1). Ohman's ten-year-old son Edward subsequently dusted
off the stone with his cap and noticed strange symbols carved
into the surface. Ohman was a migrant from Sweden, and his
neighbour Nils Flaten was from Norway, but neither guessed that
the markings might be runes. The heavy slab (202 pounds, or
92 kilos) was taken to Kensington and exhibited in the window of
a bank. Scandinavians in the local community who saw it included
a few who had seen similar markings reproduced in Scandinavian
books, and the emerging consensus was that the inscriptions on
the face and side might be runes.

Fig. 9.1 Kensington Runestone

A copy of the inscription was sent to Olaus Jensen Breda, a Norwegian professor at the University of Minnesota, where he taught Latin and Scandinavian languages. Breda was a classicist by training, and had no specialist knowledge of epigraphy or runes, but he was able to produce a rough translation, apart from the numerals. His conclusion was that the stone was a harmless spoof made by a prankster who took pleasure in the prospect of deceiving a professor.

At about the same time, a transcription was sent to George Oliver Curme Sr, a Germanic philologist at Northwestern University (Evanston, Illinois), and the stone itself was subsequently shipped to him. Like Breda, he was neither an epigrapher nor a runic specialist. When the stone arrived, he was puzzled by the discrepancies between the transcription that he had been sent and the runes on the stone. He translated the latter (without the numbers), and after consulting specialists in Denmark and Norway, concurred with Breda's view that the stone was a fake. In the light of these and other adverse judgements, the stone was returned to Olof Ohman, who left it lying outside, apparently face down. It lay undisturbed until 1907, when the Norwegian-American Hjalmar Holand, who was writing a history of Norwegian settlements in America, visited the farm, and Olman gave him the stone.

Holand was to become a committed and energetic champion for the cause of the stone's authenticity. In 1908 he published his book on the settlements (in Norwegian), in which the stone had an important presence. Articles and lectures in English followed, and the Minnesota Historical Society initiated an investigation into the stone's authenticity. Holand took the stone to Europe, exhibiting it in Scandinavia and France. In 1910 the Minnesota Historical Society published its report, which after a careful review of the evidence pronounced the stone authentic. By this time several translators had managed to make sense of the numbers. Holand wrongly took the credit for being the first to do so. There are many problems concerning the precise meaning of some of the words, but one might translate the inscription

8 Götalanders and 22 Northmen on a journey of exploration from Vinland through the West. We made camp by two skerries one day's journey north from this stone. One day we were fishing. After we came home we found 10 men red with blood and dead. AVM. Save [us] from evil.

We have 10 men by the sea to look after our ships 14 days' journey from this island. Year 1362

The revelation of the date was a sensation. The public, especially the Scandinavian public, rejoiced in the discovery that a group of Nordic warriors had arrived in Minnesota in 1362, long before Columbus 'discovered' America. The implication of the letters AVM on the inscription, which could be expanded to *Ave Maria* or *Ave Virgo Maria*, were quickly welcomed by the Catholic Church. In 1909 the Most Reverend John Ireland, the inaugural Archbishop of St Paul, welcomed evidence of the early presence of Catholic Christians in America. Most local Catholics were of Czech or German origin, so the Catholic claim crossed an ethnic line as well as a confessional one.

Holand's advocacy for the stone's authenticity continued for the rest of his long life; he published his last book, *A Pre-Columbian Crusade to America,* in 1962. As he explained in his autobiography (*My First Eighty Years,* 1957), Holand

> became involved in a scholastic inquiry which has lasted half-a-century and the end is not yet. It has been my chief subject of study and meditation, about which I have written four books and more than a hundred articles in various periodicals. It necessitated three research trips to European universities and museums and each year I have made at least one trip to northwestern Minnesota to investigate new finds and circumstances.

The process of contextualizing the stone began with Holand, whose assiduous research had led him to a sixteenth-century translation (into Danish) of a decree issued in 1354 by Magnus, king of Sweden (as Magnus IV) and regent of Norway. The decree noted reports that there was apostasy among the Norse Greenlanders, and ordered an expedition led by 'Powell knudszøn' (in modern Norwegian, Pål Knutsson) to find the apostates and bring them back to the church. The decree does not mention the lands to the west of Greenland, but Holand confidently asserted that the expedition sailed west across the Davis Strait, through Hudson Strait, and then south into Hudson Bay, up the Nelson River and Red River, reaching what is now Kensington in 1362. Documents that survive only in a late translation are always suspect, so it is not altogether clear that the decree is what it purports to be—it may be a sixteenth-century forgery designed to bolster the Danish claim to Greenland, in pursuit of which Christian IV had sent three expeditions from Denmark in a vain search for the Norse Greenlanders.

Such considerations did not deter Holand, who proceeded to create a context beyond the immediate vicinity of Kensington. He identified various agricultural instruments as Norse, and also embarked on a hunt for the mooring stones to which the Norse would have secured their boats when exploring Minnesota. He found thirteen mooring stones, which were boulders in which a hole had been drilled to accommodate a ringbolt to which a painter could be secured. These stones were approximately 75 miles apart, and the happy discovery that there were thirteen of them meshed well with the assertion on the runestone that the warriors had travelled for fourteen days from the place where their ships were moored.

In 1946 Holand announced his identification of the site of the first church in America, which was a temporary chapel on the site now known as the Sauk Center Altar Rock (in northern Minnesota, near the Canadian border). He interpreted holes in boulders on the site as receptacles for wooden supports of an altar. And by counting mooring stones, he was able to establish the precise date when the expedition reached this spot. It was 15 August 1362, the Feast of the Assumption of the Virgin, and on that day the first mass was celebrated in what is now America. The Altar Rock was reconsecrated in an ecumenical (Catholic–Lutheran) ceremony in 1975, and is now promoted as a stop on the Viking Trail: fantasy history has become tourist history. In 1959 Holand introduced a new member of the cast of characters on the expedition: the Carmelite friar and astronomer Nicholas Lynn had been a member, and Holand declared that Nicolas had been the first Englishman to visit America.

Academic opinion on the authenticity of the stone was divided. The most prominent and persistent doubter was Johan Holvik, a Minnesota academic specializing in Norwegian language and literature. For the rest of their lives, Holand and Holvik were locked in a debate—at first friendly, and eventually acrimonious—about the runestone, and much of the evidence that their research uncovered was to form the basis of debate up to the present. The fortunes of the stone have oscillated throughout its history, and in the late 1940s advocates were sufficiently in the ascendant for the stone to be displayed for a year (February 1948 to February 1949) at the prestigious Smithsonian Institution in Washington, DC. The inference of the display was that the stone might be evidence of the Norse having arrived in America 130 years before Columbus. Local Catholic support for the stone continued, and in 1952 Father James Reardon, a prominent Minnesota priest, explained in his history of the diocese that if the stone be genuine, and the consensus of competent scholarly opinion points in that direction, it proves beyond reasonable doubt that Christ was in Minnesota more than a century before Columbus, that representatives of the Catholic Church, one of whom may have been a priest, were in the state in Pre-Columbian days, and that the first prayer on record on the continent was borne heavenward from the shore of one of its ten thousand lakes.

Father Reardon was not a crank. He considered the evidence, and drew what seemed to be a reasonable conclusion. Thus is history rewritten by honest men.

In 1958 this scholarly consensus (inasmuch as it existed) was decisively shattered by the publication of *The Kensington Stone: A mystery solved*, by Erik Wahlgren, a Germanic philologist specializing in Scandinavian languages. Hjalmar Holand was still alive and active, but Wahlgren showed no mercy as he eviscerated Holand's arguments. He demonstrated that the spelling, grammar, and style were not medieval, but rather corresponded to a modern Minnesota dialect of Swedish. He showed that the orthography is highly irregular, combining runic conventions from various periods. Wahlgren did not name the hoaxer, but (following Holvik's lead) pointed out that a textbook in Olman's farmhouse contains an account of the runes on the stone, and that a scrapbook in Olman's possession contains clues to his unusual understanding of the letters AVM in the Kensington inscription. Wahlgren's work was welcomed by the scholarly community, but excoriated in Minnesota, where he could safely be dismissed as an out-of-state interloper, possibly on the payroll of the Knights of Columbus.

Ten years later another attack on the Kensington Runestone was published, this time by Theodore Blegen, a native of Minnesota who had risen to become dean of the Graduate School at the University of Minnesota. Blegen painstakingly documented the circumstances surrounding the discovery and the status of the stone in the years that followed. His archival work usefully complemented Wahlgren's philological investigation, and his conclusion that the inscription was a hoax looked set to bury the controversy permanently. It did indeed mark the low point in the fortunes of the stone, but thereafter its popular reputation rose steadily.

In the concluding paragraph of his book, Wahlgren had expressed the hope that 'this classic hoax be restored to dignity as a permanent exhibit at Alexandria, where visitors from afar will witness, not an ancient runic monument, but a memorial to the pioneer settlers of Douglas County'. This hope of permanent display in Alexandria was realized while Wahlgren's book was in production. The Runestone Museum opened in 1958, with the stone as its sole exhibit. Four years later, 1962 was celebrated as the 600th anniversary of the episode inscribed on the stone. The celebrations included a Runestone Pageant commissioned from a local historian and theatre professional called Bert Merling, who wrote, directed, and narrated the pageant. The pageant and the published text were sponsored by the Alexandria Jaycees—not the elders of the community, but the young professionals in the Junior Chamber of Commerce. Hjalmar Holand seems not to have attended (he was then 89 years old), but he featured as an heroic character, revered as a scholar and historian who bore brickbats from his detractors with dignity. Holand's bold defence of the authenticity of the stone echoes the bold defence of the Christian faith by King Magnus, who assembled the band of 'Christian Vikings' whose travels were to take them to Greenland, Hudson Bay, and through the river system to Kensington, where ten of their number were martyred for their faith. The arrival of the

Vikings in Minnesota is declared to the be 'the greatest historical event in American history'.

David Krueger, who has written what is (in my view) the finest of the many books on the subject of the Kensington Runestone, first brought the 1962 pageant to the attention of the scholarly community, drawing out the racial implications of the use of Wagner's music in the pageant. Krueger notes that 1962 was the centenary of the Dakota War, which played an important part in the collective memory of Minnesotans, and he has argued that that conflict may have inspired the text inscribed on the runestone. It is a commonplace (first articulated by Jim Wallace in a *Sojourners* article in 1987) that 'the United States of America was established as a white society, founded upon the near genocide of another race and then the enslavement of yet another'. The Dakota rising was certainly bloody, and some 400 white settlers were murdered by the Dakota over the loss of their land. The suppression of the uprising was even bloodier. More than 300 Dakota were sentenced to death. As the death penalty required presidential assent, Abraham Lincoln was asked to confirm the sentences. He chose to commute most of the sentences, but agreed to the execution of the thirty-eight men convicted of killing unarmed civilians. They were hanged simultaneously, in the largest mass execution in the history of America. In the brutal ethnic cleansing in the wake of the executions, the Dakota were driven out of Minnesota, and white settlers moved in. The memory of the executions was perpetuated in images that remained available for decades. In 1902 the Standard Brewing Company in Mankato (the site of the hanging) produced a commemorative tray to mark the fortieth anniversary of the execution (Fig. 9.2). This monument to bad taste is still a collector's item. It reinforces the stereotype of the

Fig. 9.2 Standard Brewing Company commemorative tray

triumph of white civilization over Indian savagery, without a thought for the dispossession that occasioned the rebellion. The memory of white Scandinavian settlers dying as martyrs is reflected in the inscription on the runestone, which documents medieval Scandinavians being slaughtered by savages. And the date on the runestone is 1362, which was 500 years before the Dakota War of 1862; as Krueger shrewdly observes, this opens the possibility that the date on the runestone is an attempt to create half a millennium of prehistory.

Fig. 9.3 Viking statue, Alexandria, Minnesota

The Runestone Museum has evolved in the sixty years since it opened. The sight that greets the visitor approaching the museum is an enormous statue of a Viking (with a winged helmet) (Fig. 9.3). The statue was made for the Minnesota pavilion at the 1964–5 World's Fair in New York, where the runestone was displayed. In New York the Viking's shield was emblazoned with the words 'Minnesota birthplace of America?'. When it returned to Minnesota, the question mark was dropped and the birthplace made more precise, so it now reads 'Alexandria birthplace of America'.

The museum across the street from the statue has a fine collection of artefacts documenting the presence in Minnesota of Native Americans and the settlement by Scandinavians. In the section of the museum devoted to the medieval Norse explorers, the runestone is complemented by some forty artefacts found in Minnesota. The museum aspires to neutrality on the authenticity of the runestone, and is openly sceptical about some of the artefacts. It claims unequivocal authenticity for only one, the medieval Climax fire steel (so called because it was found in the Minnesota town of Climax) that was previously in the collection of the University Museum in Oslo, but carefully asserts that it was 'said to be found buried in 1870'. In other cases, signage is resolutely open-minded. A 'bearded axe' found near Norway Lake, for example, is said to resemble a medieval weapon, and 'if found where said, adds to claim of authenticity for Runestone'. This is one of several artefacts given to Holand by local farmers who had recovered them along the route indicated by the mooring stones that he had discovered. One group of battleaxes identified by Holand as medieval Norse was subsequently identified as tobacco-cutters made in Ohio by the Battle Ax Tobacco Company.

The even-handed approach to the runestone means that its authenticity is regarded as unresolved, and signage explains that current research by Richard Nielsen (who died in 2016), Scott Wolter, and Henrik Williams is continuing. This bland statement obscures a bitter debate. In 2005 Dr Nielsen and Mr Wolter published a 570-page book entitled *The Kensington Rune Stone: Compelling New Evidence*. The book was self-published, and the authors candidly acknowledge that it was not subject to formal academic review. The volume is a useful documentary compendium of the history of the runestone controversy. It also sets out an expanded context for the stone, elaborating on the earlier exposition of the voyage by Holand. Codes embedded in the runes revealed that they had been carved by a Cistercian monk who accompanied the Templars on the expedition. The code also offered a clue to the location of the Holy Grail, which had been brought to America, and to the role of the Freemasons.

Most professionals in the field do not believe that the Norse were present in Minnesota in the fourteenth century, and therefore assume that the Kensington stone is a product of the nineteenth century. The only runologist with serious academic standing who managed to keep his mind open to the possibility of the stone being medieval is Henrik Williams, who is professor of Scandinavian languages at Uppsala University. Professor Williams has no sympathy for readings based on codes, but he was open to the idea that the presence of dotted 'R's in the inscription would constitute evidence that the inscription was medieval. Shortly after the *Compelling New Evidence* book was published, Professor Williams revised his view, and declared that the dots were natural features of the rock and not man-made. Dr Nielsen agreed with this revised view, but Mr Wolter did not, and this led to a very public rift. When Professor Williams visited the museum in 2010, Dr Nielsen was denied access. Words were exchanged, and subsequently the director and two board members prepared an affidavit setting out their sense of what had transpired. Professor Williams replied with a dignified statement setting out his version of events. As the matter now stands, no academic professional is prepared to endorse the authenticity of the Kensington Runestone, but its champions are confident that its antiquity has been established beyond reasonable doubt. In 2017 Scott Wolter set out the 'proof positive' that the inscription is medieval, explaining that he had discovered the first four symbolic numbers of 8, 22, 2 and 1, as they occur in sequence add up to 32, then 33, which equals the system of degrees within Scottish Rite Freemasonry. These numbers are directly related to the Hebrew mysticism of the Kabbalah that traces the same numbering system to the number of bones and nerves in the spinal cord (32) with the skull, and brain within it, totaling 33. The remaining numbers of 1, 10, 10, 14, relate to the Ten Commandments, the Enochian Legends, and the Isis/Osiris mysteries and the allegorical stories of the annual cycle of life on earth that every culture on the planet experiences. In short, the Kensington inscription is largely allegorical with certain factual information peppered in for the initiated few to decipher.

Alas, I am not numbered among the initiated few.

In the twentieth century, two more runestones were found in Minnesota, and another was found across the border in Manitoba. On 13 November 1933 the banner headline of *The Winnipeg Evening Tribune* was 'Runic Stone found near Sandy Hook'. The inscribed stone had been found near Sandy Hook, on the west side of Lake Winnipeg, a few miles south of the Icelandic community of Gimli, in the area established in 1875 as New Iceland (Nýja Ísland). The front-page story describes how local scientific groups were 'thrown into a fever of excitement by the discovery of the strange carvings on the boulder'. The runes, a local scholar explained, constituted 'testimony to the exploration of Manitoba and the Hudson Bay as far back as 1362 AD'.

In 1949 a local Minnesota newspaper, the *Elbow Lake Herald*, reported that a local farmer had found a heart-shaped runestone while laying a path near his home some five years earlier. It was initially translated '1776. Four maidens camped on this hill'. Hjalmar Holand, working from a plaster cast, translated the date as 1362. The farmer who had found the stone was confronted, and confessed to having carved the inscription as a prank.

In 1995 a boulder known as the AVM Runestone was found by a local Viking researcher near the site where the Kensington Runestone was found. The inscription was similar to the one on the Kensington Runestone. A local research group examined the stone in detail and concluded that the inscription was modern. In 2001 Robert Johnson and Janey Westin rediscovered the boulder, and decided that the inscription was genuine. Their judgement encouraged Scott Wolter and the Kensington Runestone Scientific Testing Team to examine the boulder. They cleared away lichens and found more runes, including a date of 1363, a year after the date on the Kensington Runestone. The boulder was taken to a laboratory in St Paul for analysis. On 13 August 2001 the Runestone Museum announced that the inscription was genuine, that its purpose was to mark a Norse grave, and its significance was that it constituted important evidence of the authenticity of the Kensington Runestone and evidence of a Christian presence in America long before Columbus. In October 2001, however, two academics who in the 1980s had been postgraduates in the Department of Germanic Philology at the University of Minnesota issued an affidavit saying that in 1985 they and three classmates had carved the runes with a hammer and chisel, incorporating in the inscription a magical formula, a Christian invocation and the date 1363. Undeterred, Dr Johnson and Ms Westin re-entered the fray in 2012 with their book entitled *The Last Kings of Norse America*. As I explained in the previous chapter, they used the inscriptions on the Spirit Pond Runestones and the Kensington Runestone to show that King Magnus commanded his second son, Haakon VI of Norway, to accompany the expedition led by Pål Knutsson.

In the years before he ascended to the throne, Haakon was in America, striving to restore the fur trade.

The argument about the authenticity of the runestone rumbles on. There has always been a small number of academics who have taken the view that the balance of evidence favours authenticity. In 1982, for example, the romance philologist Robert Hall published *Kensington Rune-Stone: Authentic and Important*, and in 2005 the anthropologist Alice Kehoe published a supportive account entitled *The Kensington Runestone: Approaching a Research Question Holistically*; ten years later, she wrote the sympathetic 'Foreward' to *Compelling New Evidence*.

In my view, the disciplines that have provided the decisive evidence are philology and runology. Philological research has shown that although most of the individual words can all be found in medieval charters, albeit rarely and from different parts of Scandinavia, the language of the inscription resembles the Swedish dialect spoken in nineteenth-century Minnesota more closely than any medieval dialect.

A clearer picture has emerged from runology. For more than a century advocates of the stone have tried to seek the runic forms on the Kensington stone in the 6,000 undisputedly genuine medieval runestones, and, one by one, medieval precedents have been found for disputed runes, again albeit rarely and from different parts of Scandinavia. This is an instance of confirmation bias, in which researchers investigate areas with potential to prove that their hypotheses are correct. There is, however, another corpus of runic writing, in the historic Swedish province of Dalecarlia. These runes, which remained in use until the early twentieth century, were well known to scholarship (Linnaeus had noted them in 1734), but not to students of the Kensington stone.

In 2004, however, Professor Tryggve Sköld, a researcher at the Institute for Dialectology, Onomastics and Folklore Research (a research archive in the northern Swedish city of Umeå), found two sheets of paper, dated 1883 and 1885, written by brothers called Larsson, setting out details of a runic code used by journeymen to communicate with each other. The character set is much more closely related to that of the Kensington Runestone than that of any medieval inscription. The same character set has also been found on an agricultural yoke from Månsta (Dalecarlia), dated 1907—and the Larrsson documents show that the yoke did not derive from the Kensington Runestone. This evidence means that the Kensington Runestone was carved in the nineteenth century by someone from central Sweden.

There is no evidence that enables scholars to identify the carver or carvers. It is certainly possible that Olaf Ohman was the victim of a hoax rather than its perpetrator. Without knowledge of the perpetrator, we cannot guess the motive: perhaps a prank led to a situation in which no one could confess, or perhaps mockery of Olaf Ohman or of academic experts. We can, however, draw some inferences from the extraordinary reception history of the artefact.

In Alexandria and at the site of the Ohman farm, the flame has burnt brightly ever since the stone was found. As the birthplace of America, Alexandria is more important (as Holand declared) than Plymouth Rock. In 1957 Catholic appropriation of the runestone took a step forward with the dedication of a shrine to Our Lady of the Runestone in the Catholic church in Alexandria. On Runestone Drive in Kensington, the Our Lady of the Runestone Church was consecrated in 1963. As the area had largely been settled by Lutherans, confessional polemicists tried to discredit the Catholic claim by drawing on Holvik's contention that AVM did not refer to the Blessed Virgin, but was rather an evocation of AUM (in runes the U and V are not distinguished), a Buddhist evocation of the Supreme Being that Holvik had found in a scrapbook owned by Ohman.

In recent years the authenticity and importance of the Kensington Runestone has been repeatedly affirmed in the local area. The official website of the City of Kensington affirms the existence of 'blue-eyed Mandan Indians who knew about Christianity before the first settlers arrived, and who lived in square medieval-Norwegian design buildings'. There is an annual Vikingland Band Festival in Alexandria. In January 2018 the Kensington Rune Stone Visitors Center was opened on the site of the Ohman farm.

The Kensington Runestone is also important in the larger area of Scandinavian settlement in Minnesota and the eastern part of the Dakotas. Before the discovery of the stone, Vinland had been confidently located in New England. It was satisfying to rural Minnesotans, who had been regarded as country bumpkins by sophisticated New Englanders, that the Norse had first settled in Minnesota. Eventually the urban citizens of the Twin Cities began to regard the stone as part of their heritage. In 2014 the Minnesota Fringe Festival hosted a musical called *The Ohman Stone* at a theatre in Minneapolis. The musical was written and directed by Sheridan O'Keefe, who defends the Ohman family from the slander and ridicule that they have suffered at the hands of scholars. The characters in the story of the Kensington stone are presented as ghosts, including the virtuous Hjalmar Holand and the villainous figures of Johan Holvik, Theodore Blegen, and Eric Wahlgren.

Many people in Minnesota and the eastern Dakotas continue to believe in the authenticity of the Kensington Runestone and the historicity of pre-Columbian Norse settlement in the region. Minnesota's principal football team is called the Minnesota Vikings, and the team's website explains that it is 'named after Norsemen, the Scandinavian warriors that settled modern-day Minnesota'. There is a reconstructed Viking ship in the Hjemkomst Center in Moorhead, on the border with North Dakota. In nearby Ulen, there is a Viking Sword Museum, but the artefact after which it is named (found in 1911, and identified as Viking by Hjalmar Holand) is a military sword manufactured in Philadelphia in the early nineteenth century. A 1989 study by Michael W. Hughey and Michael G. Michlovic (see Further Reading) noted that large numbers of artefacts said to be Norse are displayed in museums to which schoolchildren are taken, and the Norse are commemorated in the names of many parks and monuments. Regional Catholic endorsement constitutes support from a quarter that is usually scholarly in its assertions.

There is clearly an ethnic element in this widespread regional belief. Most purportedly Norse artefacts in America have been found in areas of Scandinavian settlement, and that is certainly true of Minnesota and the eastern Dakotas. When they first arrived, these migrants were regarded as marginal to the dominant ethnic group in America, those whose notion of America's beginning was centred on a fanciful historiography woven around the Mayflower. The Kensington Runestone offered an earlier, Scandinavian beginning—hence Alexandria as the birthplace of America. In the late twentieth century, by which time Scandinavian Americas were accepted as mainstream Americans, pride in ancestry manifested itself in ethnically themed heritage events ranging from folk festivals to courses in Scandinavian culture at local colleges and universities. The Sons of Norway, a fraternal benefit society, has many local lodges that promote Norwegian culture. Hughey and Michlovic also advance a case for small-town and rural inhabitants of the region harbouring resentment towards the powerful states of the eastern seaboard, which are deemed through their corrupt control of the economy and claims to cultural priority to be exploiting a morally superior Midwest. In such a context, the myth of blood sacrifice inscribed in the stone has more authority than a sentimental tale of the first Thanksgiving.

In the new millennium, as the region has become more diverse, ethnic nationalism has become muted in some quarters, but its voice can still be heard, albeit in a new form. Economic prosperity has increasingly been concentrated in cities, and in the declining economies of rural America there has been a resurgence of populist conservatism. 'Small town', in the common view of the cultural elites of the coasts, has ceased to signify civic virtue, and now implies provincial small-mindedness. Reaction to this demeaning caricature takes many forms, but one line of defence is the inheritance of heroic helmeted Vikings, which is celebrated in events such as the Midwest Viking Festival. Civic websites, notably that of Todd County, continue to affirm the historicity of the Norse presence in the fourteenth century. When the champions of the Norse presence encounter impediments to their belief, they manufacture evidence. One example is the awkwardness of there not being a route through which boats could have passed to Kensington. The explanation is that water levels were much higher in the fourteenth century. Some versions of this explanation have the Norse sailing across Lake Agassiz, a vast glacial lake which, when first hypothesized in the early nineteenth century, covered much of the land between Kensington and the Nelson River, which flows into Hudson Bay. The fact that the lake drained c. 8000 BCE is a difficulty often overlooked.

The challenging of the facts adduced by runestone believers is futile. It makes more sense to ask why there is so much resistance to the findings of science. The rejection of archaeological accounts of the past is of course part of a larger distrust of expert scientific opinion, as instanced in climate change denial or rejection of biological evolution, but it is also a means of supporting the ethnic identity of Minnesota citizens of Scandinavian descent. This is an issue to which I shall return in the final chapter.

CHAPTER 10

UNDERSTANDING NORSE AMERICA

W hy does the question of who discovered America arise?
Why is the discovery celebrated? Why do so many people
argue about who arrived first? And why does the Norse presence
in North America matter? Indeed, why do many Americans
continue to believe that the Norse preceded Columbus in the
United States (which Columbus never visited)? Why have
Americans paid for statues of Leif Eirikson to be erected in Iceland
and Greenland?

The seeds of the answers to such questions lie in the early
European colonization of America, and in the emergence, after
early Spanish domination, of the English as the most successful
colonial power. Looking back from the perspective of the twenty-
first century, we may legitimately wonder what could have made
the colonists feel entitled to conquer and occupy someone else's
homeland, to disinherit and force to the margins of society the
people that they displaced, and to go on to enslave the peoples of
another continent? What is the origin of this sense of superiority,
and how did it lead to a spurious historiography whereby America
was founded by Vikings? The larger context for such questions is
the process whereby a settler society creates political and
educational power structures which it then dominates, and then

fashions an imagined history in which the indigenous people are characterized as savages and marginalized with respect to land. This fiction presents northern Europeans as racially and culturally superior, and so rightful claimants of Native American lands.

The Norse crossed the North Atlantic, settling in the Atlantic archipelago, the Faroes, Iceland, and Greenland, and reaching further west to the edges of the North American mainland. There was nothing inevitable about this journey westward; no magnet was drawing the Norse to their destiny in America. The belief that the Norse were the first Europeans to come to what is now the United States has been difficult to sustain in the absence of archaeological evidence. The need to sustain the belief had a number of consequences. Leif Eirikson, a legendary figure, was hardened into a solid historical figure, the discoverer of America, and statues of Leif have been erected by Americans in Iceland (Reykjavík and Eiríksstaðir), Greenland (Qassiarsuk), and the United States (Boston, Chicago, Duluth, Milwaukee, St Paul and Seattle). A massive statue of Thorfinn Karlsefni stands in Philadelphia, but as I write (2019), it has been toppled into the river, possibly by aggrieved defenders of Columbus. Another effect of the belief that the Norse 'discovered' America is that ambiguous artefacts are tendentiously interpreted, so the Maine penny, the Newport Tower, and the mounds of Ohio and the lower Mississippi, all of which are genuine artefacts, become 'proof' of a Norse presence in America. In the case of the mounds, the notion that they are the work of Vikings serves to dispossess Native Americans by denying their relationship to the artefacts that their ancestors constructed.

Beyond these real artefacts whose significance has been distorted, there are scores of fiercely defended fake artefacts, of which the Kensington Runestone is the principal example. Fake artefacts tend to be found in areas of Scandinavian settlement, which implies that they may be expressions of ethnic pride by migrants. This is entirely understandable, and can be relatively harmless. In the nineteenth century, Scandinavian migrants were marginal Americans; their claim to arrival prior to the English (and the Spanish) is entirely spurious, but is nonetheless a mechanism for claiming legitimacy. Such pride in an ethnic minority only becomes sinister when it leads to affirmations of ethnic superiority. At the extreme, there were sympathisers in the United States with the Aryan supremacy claimed by the Nazis; their numbers included Charles Lindbergh and other members of the America First Committee. Similarly, in Canada the *Parti National Social Chrétien* supported Nazi theories of race. It is inappropriate, however, to see the racial theories of the nineteenth and early twentieth century, repugnant though they were, through the prism of the Holocaust, even though that was where they ultimately led. For the purposes of understanding the notion that the Vikings settled in America, it is more useful to consider the origins of the idea, which lay in exceptionalism, nineteenth-century science, and the process by which Anglo-Saxons came to consider themselves as descendants of the Norse.

American exceptionalism is rooted in an earlier English exceptionalism. The attitude of the poet and polemicist John Milton is typical of early modern English convictions. Milton thought, for example, that the Reformation could not have been ignited by Luther, because Luther had the misfortune to be a foreigner. When God speaks, Milton explained, he speaks first to his Englishmen. On this understanding, the true father of the Reformation was not Luther, but Wyclif, who thereby became the first Protestant. Such claims are endearingly batty, but they have a darker side, in that they slowly evolve into the notion that white Anglo-Saxon Protestants are the chosen of God. WASPs, on this reading, enjoy a privilege that has divine authority. Such assumptions have disfigured Anglophone societies through the centuries, and in the twenty-first century still retain a sinister attraction.

The idea of the Anglo-Saxon and the notion of Anglo-Saxon superiority have their beginnings in a myth of origin developed in the course of the English Reformation. The church from which England had broken was not represented as catholic (in the sense of 'universal') but as Roman, and therefore foreign. The nefarious influence of this foreign church was deemed to have begun with the Norman invasion in 1066, which corrupted the pre-Norman Anglo-Saxon church. Pursuit of this claim led to scholarly investigation of the Anglo-Saxon church. The most important patron of such scholarship was Matthew Parker, Archbishop of Canterbury from 1559 to 1575, who in his final years devoted tracts of time to the construction of a historical foundation for the Church of England. He amassed an immensely important library (now largely in the keeping of Corpus Christi College, Cambridge) with a view to demonstrating that the English church was not new, but rather a revival of a proto-Protestant Anglo-Saxon church, now purged of Romish accretions and corruption.

The scholarly movement led by Archbishop Parker had a polemical dimension in the work of the Protestant martyrologist John Foxe, whose *Acts and Monuments* (informally known as the *Book of Martyrs* since its first publication in 1563) contended that the English were a chosen people, an elect nation who had thrown off the Papist yoke, and the inheritors of a church that could trace its origins (via Wyclif, the first Protestant) to Joseph of Arimathea, who, after he buried Jesus, travelled to England and founded the English church at Glastonbury. As this story evolved, Joseph was said to have travelled to England repeatedly before his final journey, and to have taken with him his nephew, the boy Jesus. This tradition has been encapsulated in the hymn 'Jerusalem':

> And did those feet in ancient time / Walk upon England's mountains green? And was the holy Lamb of God / On England's pleasant pastures seen?

The distinctly ahistorical notion of Jesus visiting England has a parallel embedded in the *Book of Mormon*, which describes Jesus visiting America shortly after his resurrection. Both are products of exceptionalism.

The idea of the Anglo-Saxon chosen by God intersected in complex ways with the developing northern European myth of the antiquity of the Germanic peoples, which in the closing decades of the sixteenth century was underpinned by the availability (from 1575) of Tacitus's *Germania*, a short tract destined to have a malign influence up to the twentieth century, when Himmler appropriated it to support Nazi theories of race. In England the principal champion of Tacitus was Richard Rowlands, an exiled Catholic writer and intelligence agent who published under his grandfather's surname of Verstegan. His influential work of Anglo-Saxon antiquarian scholarship was called *A Restitution of Decayed Intelligence* (1605), an account of the origins of 'the most noble and renowned English nation' in which the thin trickle of English blood in the veins of the avowedly Scottish James I of England (who was a great-great-grandson of Henry VII, who was half-Welsh) was deemed sufficient for him to be declared by

Verstegan to be 'descended of the chiefest blood royal of our ancient English-Saxon kings'. The English people, who in Verstegen's view had to be distinguished from the British people (the descendants of ancient Britons), were deemed to be Germanic Saxons of exemplary character.

Thomas Jefferson, ever willing to turn his compendious learning to the cause of the new republic, exalted the Saxons. His suggestion for the Great Seal, for example, was a representation of 'Hengist and Horsa, the Saxon chiefs, from whom we claim the honour of being descended, and whose political principles and form of government we have assumed'. Elsewhere, he asked,

> Has not every restitution of the ancient Saxon laws had happy effects? Is it not better now that we return at once into that happy system of our ancestors, the wisest and most perfect ever yet devised by the wit of man, as it stood before the eighth century?

The myth of an America rooted in Anglo-Saxon England enabled white colonists in the revolutionary period to see themselves as a people whose love of liberty had ancient precedent.

The idea of a pure Anglo-Saxon race favoured of God was transmitted to America by the puritan separatists who migrated to America to establish theocratic colonies. In the modern United States, they have been mythologized as pilgrims (which they weren't) fleeing persecution (which they weren't), and the expansion to the west that followed the initial settlements has been treated as providential. In an appendix to his *Attempt to shew that America must be known to the ancients* (1773) by an 'American Englishman' (Samuel Mather), the author observes that '*Colonies, from the Beginning of Things, after the Flood, to this Day, have almost constantly led forth from the East to the West*, and not in the contrary Direction'. Mather goes on to cite an anecdote from a contemporary called Jeremy White, who was asked

> *What he thought of these* American Regions? After a little Pause he asked the Enquirer, *Whence the wise Men came, who repaired to Judea, in order to shew their Respect and pay their Homage to* the glorious King of the World? To which Question it was answered by the Gentleman, at whose House he then was, *Why, Sir, from the East*: Whereupon Mr. *White* remarked, *And let me tell You, Sir, They have been travelling Westward ever since*: And then he went on and gave it as his Judgment, that this Part of the World *seemed to him to be reserved in Providence for the* great Seat of Empire and Religion and the Theatre of considerable Events before the End of the World.

The conquest of America, and the westward expansion of the colonists, is construed as the work of Providence. The notion of a 'manifest destiny' first appeared in an editorial in the *Democratic Review* of 1845, in which Americans were urged to unite around 'the fulfillment of our manifest destiny to overspread the continent allotted by Providence for the free development of our yearly multiplying millions'.

The conflation of the Anglo-Saxons and the Norse began in the seventeenth century. Robert Molesworth (later Viscount Molesworth), who served as ambassador to Denmark for King William III, published *An account of Denmark* (1693), an attack on the Danish monarchy in which he contrasted the present with an idealized past. In this imagined past, the people of England, Germany, and Scandinavia are said to have enjoyed a commonality of freedom denied to Mediterranean people. Lord Molesworth thought in terms of peoples, not races. In the course of the next century, however, there was a gradual shift towards racial distinctions. Paul Henri Mallet, the Genevan student of Danish antiquities, wrote (in French) an account of Scandinavian history and literature which soon appeared in a heavily edited English edition as *Northern Antiquities: Or, An Historical Account of the Manners, Customs, Religion and Laws, Maritime Expeditions and Discoveries, Language and Literature of the Ancient Scandinavians* (1770). Its editor was the bishop and antiquary Thomas Percy, whose prominence in literary and courtly circles ensured a wide readership by an audience that had developed a taste for ancient poetry stimulated by the publication in the previous decade of James Macpherson's Ossian poems, Thomas Gray's verse translation of Norse poems, and Percy's own *Five Pieces of Runic Poetry*.

It was Mallet, as mediated by Percy, who facilitated the shift from culture to race. Mallet, taking his lead from Tacitus and Molesworth, had exalted the Scandinavian and Germanic tribes, but his conflation of Scandinavians and Celts was corrected by Percy, who distinguished sharply between the freedom-loving people of England, Germany, and Scandinavia, and the indifference to freedom that rendered Celtic people inferior. The Normans, from this perspective, were not French, but rather French-speaking Norse, and the Danish occupation of Anglo-Saxon England was simply the settlement of one part of the Germanic world by people of common ancestry. The various strands of the Germanic peoples were united in England. This model of ethnic descent could not accommodate the notion of the Norman yoke, and ambivalence about the Normans persisted.

In the nineteenth century, the idea of the Anglo-Saxon people as the most distinguished branch of the supreme race hardened into a racial narrative that by twenty-first century standards is repugnant. The apogee of the racial narrative came with Thomas Carlyle. Just as Disraeli was able to overlook his Jewish roots when championing Anglo-Saxonism, so Carlyle was able to repudiate his Celtic roots by declaring Scotland to be a Norse country and explaining in the first of his *Lectures on Heroes* (1841) that 'the Speech of the common people is still in a singular degree Icelandic; its Germanism has still a peculiar Norse tinge. They too are "Normans", Northmen'. Speaking about 'the strange phenomenon called over-population' in his essay on Chartism (1840), Carlyle declared, 'and yet, if this small rim of Europe is overpeopled, does not everywhere else a whole vacant Earth as it were, call to us, Come and till me, come and reap me!'. The invitation, in part because the echo of 'rape' in 'reap', sounds sexual. Just as, in the words of Charles Kingsley quoted at the outset of this book, the 'Anglo-Saxon (a female race) required impregnation by the great male race—the Norse', so the vacant earth, in the form of an unpopulated America, needed to be seeded by Anglo-Saxons.

Carlyle's 'vacant Earth' evokes the evolving legal notion of *terra nullius* (nobody's land), which originated in the Roman legal concept of *res nullius* (nobody's thing), which referred to things not owned until they were possessed (e.g. the fish in the sea). In the fifteenth century, as Europeans began to claim land outside Europe, a legal rationale was needed, and this was supplied in a series of papal bulls, the most important of which was *Romanus Pontifex* (promulgated in 1454). Pope Nicholas V, writing to King Afonso V of Portugal, set out the right of Christians to capture and enslave infidels and pagans, to seize their land and their possessions, and to turn these people and territories to their own use and profit. This right of conquest was eventually to be adopted in countries not within the papal jurisdiction, including America.

The principle underlying *Romanus Pontifex,* that only Christians could own land, had a long afterlife, so in America in 1792 Jefferson argued that the prerogatives of the Discovery Doctrine had been transferred from the British crown to the United States government. The doctrine became enshrined in common law in Johnson v. M'Intosh (1823), which articulated the principle that ownership of land lay with the government whose citizens occupied territory whose inhabitants were not subjects of a Christian monarch. Seven years later the doctrine was enshrined in statute in the Indian Removal Act (1830), which deemed that Europeans could own land, but Native Americans could only possess it.

The 'scientific' foundation of the racial hierarchy that underlay the right to dispossess had been laid by a Swede: Carl Linnaeus. In the tenth edition of *Systemae Naturae,* published in 1758, Linnaeus refined his division of the human species that he had named *homo sapiens* into four continental subspecies (Americanus, Asiaticus, Africanus, and Europaeus) by associating each race with characteristics derived from the classical 'humours' (i.e. temperaments). Americanus, in the west, was red, choleric, and upright in posture (Latin: *rufus, cholericus, rectus*). Europaeus, in the north, was white, sanguine, and muscular (Latin: *albus, sanguineus, torosus*). Asiaticus, in the east, was yellow, melancholy, and rigid (Latin: *luridus, melancholicus, rigidus*). Africanus, in the south, was black, phlegmatic, and relaxed (Latin: *niger, phlegmaticus, laxus*). This is racism raised to the dignity of science, elevated by its articulation in Latin.

The taxonomy proposed by Linnaeus was refined by the German medical scientist Johann Friedrich Blumenbach, who coined the term 'Caucasian' to denote the 'white' race that he thought originated in the Caucasus. His scheme of five races

(Caucasian, Mongolian, Malayan, Ethiopian, and American), first published in 1793, became the accepted wisdom of race theory until the mid nineteenth century. In America this taxonomy was taken up by the craniologist Samuel Morton (*Crania Americana*, 1839), who, on the basis of his examination of hundreds of skulls (which he filled with seeds and shot to measure volume), characterized Native Americans as cunning, deceitful, and vengeful, and without an aptitude for civilization.

This 'scientific' denigration of Native Americans was accompanied by an ever-increasing body of work confirming the superiority of the Anglo-Saxon branch of the Caucasian race. This 'science' touched on an issue that was also topical in terms of contemporary debate about the standing of the Bible in understanding the creation of humans. The Genesis account of human creation implied monogenesis: God's creation of a single race descended from Adam and Eve. The rival theory, championed by Morton and his contemporaries, was polygenesis: the view that the different races were separate creations. It took very considerable intellectual acrobatics to reconcile polygenesis with the accounts in Genesis of the creation of Adam and Eve and of the 'table of nations' (Genesis 10), which describes the dispersion of Noah's progeny.

Charles Darwin's subversion of the Biblical account relegated the work of Morton's generation to the dustbin of history, but there were nonetheless continuities. Monogenesis, for example, lives on in the twenty-first century in the view that humankind descended from common ancestors in Africa. Darwin also preserved elements of racial theory, so in the *Descent of Man*, he presented Celts as inferior to Anglo-Saxons. Darwin's friend (and second cousin) Francis Galton developed a new science that he termed 'eugenics', which he proclaimed in a book entitled *Hereditary Genius* (1869), which was to become the starting point of Nazi theories of race.

On both sides of the Atlantic, the notion of an Anglo-Saxon race fortified by Viking blood gradually coalesced into an ideology that was reflected and refracted in the literary and historical writing of the period. In Disraeli's *Sybil* (1845), the heroine is allowed to overcome impediments to her marriage to an aristocrat because of her discovery that she descends from Saxon nobles. In *Tancred* (1847), Disraeli uses Sidonia to acknowledge that a superior race, 'a Saxon race, protected by an insular position, has stamped its diligent and methodic character on the century'. The fact that a distinguished Anglican convert from Judaism should espouse Anglo-Saxon racial superiority attests to the power of the myth, but also served Disraeli's political purpose of linking the Whig aristocracy to the Normans who had displaced the noble Anglo-Saxon heritage of England. In Britain, the annexation of the figure of the seafaring Viking to the maritime Anglo-Saxon race reached its pinnacle in the imperial yarns of R. M. Ballantyne, the Scottish author of *The Coral Island*, particularly his *The Norsemen in the West, or America before Columbus* (1872). In America, Ballantyne's counterparts included Ottilie Liljencrantz, whose trilogy of Vinland novels (1902–6) for young readers extolled 'the mighty Anglo-Saxon race' and presented lightly fictionalized but wholly recognisable elements of Viking myth such as the Newport Tower.

Similar assumptions are apparent in historical writing. The preface to Benjamin Franklin DeCosta's *The Pre-Columbian Discovery of America by the Northmen* (1868) exhorts the reader to remember that in vindicating the Northmen we honor those who not only gave us the first knowledge possessed of the American Continent, but to whom we are indebted for much beside that we esteem valuable. In reality we fable in a great measure when we speak of our 'Saxon inheritance.' It is rather from the Northmen that we have derived our vital energy, our freedom of thought, and, in a measure that we do not yet suspect, our strength of speech.

The passage equivocates between a biological inheritance and a cultural one, possibly because De Costa's Mediterranean ancestry leads him to nudge the argument towards the cultural so that he can be part of the 'we' that shares the inheritance.

Such literature was part of a larger cultural movement known as the Viking Revival, which was inaugurated in the United States by the publication in 1837 by the Danish philologist C. C. Rafn of the weighty *Antiquitates Americanæ, sive scriptores septentrionales rerum ante-Columbianarum* ('Antiquities of America, or the writings of the historians of the north about pre-Columbian America'). Rafn, as I explained in chapter 8, was an important contributor to the claims made for Dighton Rock and the Newport Tower, but his work had a wider significance, in that it provided the scholarly foundation for the widespread view that the Norse had settled in America for three centuries. This learned volume, in which the Norse sagas were translated into Danish and Latin, was helpfully furnished with an English summary for the benefit of American readers. Rafn treated the sagas as historical accounts, and, uninhibited by the fact that he had never visited America (and never would), he confidently identified the Norse landfalls in America.

Rafn's learned treatise was soon mediated for the public by the Irish antiquarian North Ludlow Beamish, who, recognizing that Rafn's work was rendered inaccessible to most book buyers by cost and language barriers, published an abridged version called

The Discovery of America by the Northmen (1841). Beamish's purpose was not simply to mediate Rafn's treatise to the general public, but also to appropriate it to advance the prior claims of the Irish to have discovered America (his subtitle was *'with notes on the early settlement of the Irish in the Western Hemisphere'*). Beamish seized on an occasional references to Hvítramannaland ('White Man's Land') which the Norse sources cited by Rafn identified as Great Ireland (*Irland it mikla*), located in the west, near Vinland the Good (*þat liggr vestr í haf nær Vínlanndi enu góða*), to advance his view that the American mainland was known to the Norse as 'White Man's Land' or 'Greater Ireland'.

The mediation of Beamish facilitated appropriation in the American South of the notion of America as a land of white men. The antebellum novelist William Gilmore Simms, a prominent advocate of slavery, affirmed in his 'Four periods of American History' the truth of Rafn's claim to 'the first discovery and partial settlement of America by the Northmen', whom he described as 'the fierce Viking of the northern ocean'. And in an essay on 'The Discoveries of the Northmen', Simms identified the White Man's Land with 'our own dearly beloved region of South Carolina and Georgia'. Such sentiments have lived on up to the present. One example is the Battle of Liberty Place monument (displayed in New Orleans until 2017), which inscribed in stone the view that the presidential election of 1876, which marked the end of Reconstruction (the attempt to transform the Confederate states), 'recognised white supremacy in the South and gave us our state'.

The principal popularizer of the notion that Vikings were the first Europeans to settle in America was Rasmus Anderson, who was professor of Scandinavian studies at University of

Wisconsin–Madison. In 1874 he published *America Not Discovered by Columbus*, which had a mixed reception from academic readers but proved to be very popular with the wider public. Anderson's lobbying led in 1929 to the proclamation of Leif Erikson Day in Wisconsin. The observance spread to other states, and in 1964 Congress authorized President Lyndon Johnson to proclaim 9 October as Leif Erikson Day. In Anderson's view, the spirit of the Norsemen

> found its way into the Magna Carta of England and the Declaration of Independence in America. The spirit of the Vikings still survives in the bosoms of Englishmen, Americans and Norsemen, extending their commerce, taking bold positions against tyranny, and producing wonderful internal improvements in their countries.

In Anderson's view, the Norse discovery of America, far from being inconsequential, led to the creation of all that was good in the character of the modern American. His notion that Scandinavian and English migrants descended from the same stock was an important mechanism for placing Scandinavian migrants at the heart of a country dominated by citizens of English ancestry. The idea of Americans as successors of the Vikings lives on: opening the Smithsonian's exhibition *Vikings: The North Atlantic Saga* in 2000, Hillary Clinton argued that 'the Vikings, after all, are more than an historical presence in North America; they also represent the spirit of discovery that Americans, especially, can relate to'.

Anderson's student Hjalmal Holand, the tireless advocate of the Kensington Runestone, often promoted Norse priority by distinguishing the proto-Protestant Scandinavians from the perfidious Spanish. The distinction between eirenic northern Europeans, who were settlers, and the brutal Spanish, who were conquistadors, led him to deprecate Columbus. In Holand's view, the Norse had come in peace as Christians, but Columbus came with the eyes of a thief, seeing America only for its potential for pillage.

Promotion of the myth of Norse America took myriad forms. In 1882 the heiress Catharine Lorillard Wolfe commissioned a 'cottage' on the shore at Newport Rhode Island, home of the famed the 'Norse' tower. This substantial mansion, named 'Vinland', was decorated on the exterior with Celtic, Nordic, and runic symbols, and on one corner the roof supported the figurehead of a Viking ship. The highlight of the interior was a stained glass window with nine panels celebrating the Norse discovery of America; the window was commissioned from Morris and Company and designed by Edward Burne-Jones. Other ladies of the Golden Age could purchase Viking Revival furniture from Tiffany and Company, such as a lady's dressing table in which the vertical shafts were narwhal tusks.

The Norse discovery of America gradually became settled fact in the minds of the public, but school textbooks tended to be less dogmatic. One example is Thomas Bonaventure Lawes' *A Primary History of the United States* (1905, and in print until 1934), which was 'intended to meet the needs of a beginner's history for the elementary classes of the schools'. The first chapter ('The Indians') is a sympathetic account of Native American customs. The second chapter, entitled 'The White Men reach America', explains that,

> so far as is known, the first white men to reach America were the Northmen. This was almost one thousand years ago....One of their number, Leif Ericson, is supposed to have reached the northeast coast of America ....No one, however, knows his landing place, and no lasting results came from these voyages of the Northmen

Fig. 10.1 *The Landing of the Norsemen*

This account is illustrated by a picture of the 'Landing of the Norsemen' (Fig. 10.1). The illustration has none of the tentativeness of 'so far as is known', and firmly plants the Norse landing in the minds of its young readers.

The notion that the United States is in its essence a country whose people are primarily of Protestant northern European origin was reflected in the changes in American immigration law effected in the Johnson-Reed Act of 1924. The act restricted migration from Africa, the Middle East, and Asia, and also set limits on migrants from southern and eastern Europe. Between 1880 and 1924, four million Italians and two million Eastern European Jews migrated to America. The 1924 act imposed a quota of 4,000 a year on Italians, and quotas for countries with significant Jewish populations were similarly reduced. The climate of opinion that underlay this legislation was fertile ground for the promotion of an America with Viking origins. That promotion reached its apex the following year, when President Coolidge, speaking at the Norse-American Centennial in Falcon Heights, Minnesota, declared to roars of approval Leif Eirikson to be the discoverer of America.

In the decades that followed, Scandinavian communities assimilated, and the need for myths of origin and first contact declined. They live on, however, in communities with entrenched views on the authenticity of local relics, and in television programmes. In 2009 the History Channel broadcast a two-hour programme entitled 'Holy Grail in America' centred on Scott Wolter's contention that the runic inscription on the Kensington Runestone shows that the Vikings (accompanied by Knights Templar) preceded Columbus in America. A subsequent series called *America Unearthed*, hosted by Dr Wolter, contained an episode on 'Vikings in America'(2013). The myth of Norse America lives on.

In Conclusion

The Norse gradually expanded across the North Atlantic, settling the Faroes and Iceland permanently, and settling in Greenland for 500 years. The settlers were peasants who forged a living from hunting and farming. In the course of their long residence in Greenland, they sometimes travelled further to the west, to the edge of what is now Canada. The archaeological record shows that they sailed in the high Arctic and established what seems to be a transit camp on the northern tip of Newfoundland. They may have established a short-lived settlement on the mainland of North America, but no evidence of such a settlement has been found.

The Norse sagas seem to contain memories of travel to the west of Greenland, and of occasional encounters with the indigenous peoples that the Norse lumped together as skrælings. On the strength of this frail evidence, many Americans have elaborated this evidence of first contact into a myth centred on the idea that the descendants of the British settlers who now dominate America inherit their strength and vigour and love of freedom from the Vikings who 'discovered' America. These are wholly imagined Vikings, whose malleability to reflect racial narratives has led Annette Kolodny, author of the authoritative study of the subject, to describe them as 'plastic Vikings'. The notion that these Vikings settled in America is a legitimizing myth, fortified by distorted history and fake artefacts.

This sense of a racially and culturally superior identity, consisting of a fusion of Anglo-Saxon and Viking blood, has been deemed to justify the appropriation of the homeland of indigenous peoples in the nineteenth century, the discrimination against Irish, Italian, and Jewish migrants in the twentieth, and the continued marginalization of Americans of African and Hispanic origin in the twenty-first. The notion that true Americans are the descendants of English settlers whose character has been fortified by the admixture of Viking blood is abetted by the founding myth of Norse America.

GLOSSARY

The Old Norse Latin alphabet, which has been standardized in the scholarly literature since the nineteenth century, has several letters and diacriticals not used in modern English. The sound of thorn, or þorn (þ), resembles an initial 'th' in English (e.g. thin); the sound of eth, or eð (ð), resembles a terminal 'th' in English (e.g. both). The ǫ, which is variously known as the 'o caudata' or 'o ogonek' (both mean 'o with a little tail'), represents a nasal pronunciation; as ǫ was not included in pre-electronic character sets, it is represented (in this book as elsewhere) by ö. An acute accent is used to denote a long vowel.

1. Old Norse Terms

Alþingi (anglicized as Althing) 'general assembly'. The Icelandic assembly established in 930 at Þingvellir (45 km east of Reykjavík), and the Greenlandic assembly at Gardar. The form þing ('assembly') is sometimes used for assemblies in Norse territories such as Orkney, Shetland, and the Faroes.

búð (plural **búðir**, sometimes anglicized as 'booth'). The singular form denotes a seasonal dwelling, characteristically with permanent turf walls and a covering of cloth or skin.

einfœtingr a uniped (a creature with one foot).

goði (anglicized as gothi, plural **goðar**, feminine singular **gyðja**) in early use denoted a priest, but in the Christian period, a chieftain.

knörr an ocean-going cargo ship (wider, deeper and shorter than a longship). The only substantially complete example is in the Viking Ship Museum in Roskilde.

landnám 'land-take'. In Iceland and Greenland, the land claimed by chieftains for settlement.

GLOSSARY

lögmaðr (or **lögsögumaðr**) 'lawman' or 'law speaker' at the Alþingi.

saga (plural **sögur**) anonymous narrative prose compositions, written in Iceland or Norway. The Icelandic sagas (*Íslendingasögur*) are one of the genres within this corpus.

þrall (anglicized as thrall, feminine **ambátt**): slave.

vaðmál (anglicized as vadmal) a coarse woollen cloth. The distinctive *vaðmál* woven by Norse Greenlandic women had more weft threads than warp threads (possibly for extra warmth), and so can be used to identify Greenlandic cloth at remote sites.

vínvið ('grape trees') in the sagas, either a mythical species, or the trees around which wild grape vines wound.

2. People

The surname is a relatively recent phenomenon and in the Middle Ages did not exist. People had one name and were distinguished from those who shared their names by bynames indicative of parentage or occupation or place of origin. This tradition has persisted in Iceland, where most people are listed in official documents (e.g. voting registers) by their first names, followed by a patronymic: 'son' or 'dóttir'. In some cases medieval Icelanders were known by an epithet. Thus, in the sagas, the figure known in English as Eirik the Red is identified both by that term (Eiríkr hinn rauði) and as Thorvald's son (Eiríkr Þorvaldsson)

Adalbert (c. 1000–1072) archbishop of Hamburg and bishop of Bremen.

Adam of Bremen (German: Adam von Bremen) eleventh-century German chronicler, the author of *Gesta Hammaburgensis ecclesiae ponticum* ('Deeds of the Bishops of Hamburg'), of which book 4, *Descriptio insularum aquilonis*, ('Description of the Northern Islands') is an account of the history and geography of Scandinavia and the Baltic.

Ari Thorgilsson (Icelandic: Ari Þorgilsson), also known as Ari the Wise (Ari hinn fróði) (1067–1148) Icelandic chronicler and priest, the author of *Íslendingabók*.

Bjarni Grímolfsson an Icelandic sea captain whose ship is said in the *Saga of Eirik the Red* to have become infected with maggots in the

Greenland Sea. Half the crew sailed away in the ship's boat, but the other half, including Bjarni, went down with the ship.

Bjarni Herjolfsson an Icelandic merchant captain. In the *Saga of the Greenlanders* he is blown off course while sailing to Greenland, and sees the wooded coast of Markland.

Björn Gilsson bishop of Hólar from 1147 to 1162.

Brand Saemundsson (Norse: Brandr Sæmundsson; Icelandic: Brandur Sæmundsson) bishop of Hólar from 1163 to 1201.

Eirik Gnupsson (Norse: Eiríkr Gnúpsson) first bishop of Gardar (fl. 1121).

Eirik Thorvaldsson (Norse: Eiríkr Þorvaldsson), also known as Eirik the Red (Norse: Eiríkr hinn rauði). In the Vinland Sagas, Eirik was the founder of the Norse colonies in Greenland.

Freydis Eiríksdottir Eirik the Red's daughter by an unknown mother; married to Thorvard (Norse: Þorvaldr; patronymic unknown), owner of a large farm in Gardar.

Grim Kamban (Norse: Grímr; Faroese: Grímur) in the (fragmentary) *Saga of the Faroe Islanders* (*Færeyinga Saga*), the first Norse settler in the Faroe Islands.

Gudrid Thorbjarnardottir (Norse: Guðríðr Þorbjarnardóttir; modern Icelandic: Guðríður Víðförla Þorbjarnardóttir) the Christian wife of Thorstein Eiriksson, and, after his death, Thorsten Karlsefni. Her epithet, Víðförla, (by which she is known in Iceland) means 'far-travelled'.

Gudbrand Thorlaksson (modern Icelandic: Guðbrandur Þorláksson) bishop of Hólar from 1571 to 1627.

Gunnbjörn Ulfsson Norse settler in Iceland who, according to the *Book of Settlements*, was the first person to sight Greenland.

Haki and Hekla In the *Saga of Eirik the Red*, the Scottish slaves of Thorfinn Karlsefni.

Ivar Bardarson (Norse: Ívar Bárðarson) a Norse Greenlander who lived and worked at Gardar. He was the author of a 'Description of Greenland' (c. 1360).

Ketil Thorsteinson (Icelandic: Ketil Þorsteinsson) bishop of Hólar from 1122 to 1145.

Leif Eirikson (Norse: Leifr Eiríksson), also known as Leif the Lucky (Norse: Leifr hinn heppni) son of Eirík the Red and Thorvaldsson. The epithet 'Lucky' refers to a personal quality, not to fortunate experiences.

Olaf Tryggvesson (c. 965–1000) king of Norway from 995 to 1000, instrumental in the conversion of the Norse to Christianity.

Snæbjörn Galti Holmsteinsson Icelandic seaman credited with the first intentional voyage to Greenland, c. 978.

Snorri Thorbrandson (Norse: Snorri Þorbrandsson) Icelandic merchant who accompanied Thorfinn Karlsefni to Greenland and Vinland.

Snorri Thorfinnson (Norse: Snorri Þorfinnsson), also known as Snorri Karlsefnisson, the son of Thorfinn Karlsefni and Gudrid Thorbjarnardóttir, said to be the first European child born in the Vinland colony.

Sweyn II Estridsson (Norse: Sveinn Ástríðarson; Danish: Svend Estridsen) (1019–1076) English-born King of Denmark, ruled 1047–74.

Thjodhild Jorundardottir (Norse: Þjóðhildr Iorunðardóttir), wife of Eirik the Red and mother of Thorstein and Leif.

Thorbjörg (Norse: Þorbjörg Lítilvölva) a female prophet (*völva*) in the *Saga of Eirik the Red*.

Thórdur Thorlaksson (Icelandic: Þórður Þorláksson) Lutheran bishop of Shálholt from 1674 to 1697.

Thorfinn Karlsefni Thordarson (Norse: Þorfinnr Karlsefni Þórðarson) Icelandic owner of a merchant ship, and the second husband of Gudrid Thorbjarnardóttir. In the Vinland Sagas, Thorfinn established a colony at Hop, in Vinland. He is often known by his epithet 'Karlsefni', which means 'manly'.

Thorhall (Norse: Þorhallr Veiðiman) a companion of Eirik the Red; his epithet Veidiman means 'hunter'.

Thorlak Runolfsson (Norse: Þorlákr Runólfsson; Icelandic: Þorlákur Runólfsson) bishop of Shálholt from 1118 to 1133.

Thorstein Eirikson (Norse: Þórsteinn Eiríksson) son of Eirik the Red and Thjodhild. He was the first husband of Gudrid Thorbjarnardottir.

Thorvald Eirikson (Norse: Þorvaldr Eiriksson) Eirik the Red's son by an unknown mother. He travelled to Vinland with his half-brother Leif. On a subsequent voyage he was killed in Vinland.

Tyrkir (Norse: Tyrkir Suðrmaðr) German slave of Leif, whom he accompanied to Vinland, where he found wild grapes. His epithet means 'the Southerner'.

3. Peoples

Beothuk the descendants of the aboriginal inhabitants of Newfoundland, who arrived in the first century CE. The Beothuk culture formed c. 1500 CE, and was extinct by the 1830s.

Dorset people a late Tuniit culture, active c. 500 BCE to 1500 CE, named after Cape Dorset (on Baffin Island), where their remains were first identified. There is evidence that they traded with the Greenlandic Norse.

Eskimo the term formerly used to describe the peoples of the Arctic; it is no longer acceptable in popular usage (except in Siberia), but Palaeo-Eskimo survives as a technical term in archaeology and linguistics. The indigenous inhabitants of Arctic Alaska are now known as Iñupiat. In Canada and Greenland, Inuit is the preferred term.

Indian the term has been displaced in Canada by First Nations (which does not include Inuit and Métis) and in the United States by Native American, but retains a presence in institutions such as the Smithsonian's National Museum of the American Indian. In Canada members of First Nations self-identify by their nation (Cree, Mohawk, etc.).

Innu (French: Montagnais) the aboriginal inhabitants of Labrador and north-eastern Quebec, for which the Innu name is Nitassinan. Their language is part of the Cree group, and so unrelated to Inuktitut.

Inuit (singular Inuk) the present inhabitants of the Canadian Arctic, Greenland, and Alaska. They are descendants of the Thule people.

Kalaallit the endonym used by the Western Greenlandic Inuit. The Kalaallit are descendants of the Thule people, not of the Greenlandic Dorset people.

Norse (Scandinavian: *Norroen*) the inhabitants of medieval Denmark, Greenland, Iceland, the Faroes, Norway, and Sweden; some were pirates or traders or raiders (see 'Vikings'), but most were hunters or farmers.

Skræling (Norse: skrælingi, plural skrælingar) a pejorative term used in the sagas to denote the aboriginal peoples encountered by the Norse in Greenland, Helluland, Markland, and Vinland, including the Dorset and Thule peoples, and possibly the Innu. The etymology of the term is uncertain.

Thule a proto-Inuit culture originating in Alaska c. 1000 CE, and expanding eastwards across Canada, reaching north-west Greenland c. 1300. The Thule displaced the earlier Dorset people in both the Canadian

Arctic and Greenland. There is evidence that they traded with the Greenlandic Norse. Their descendants are today's Inuit.

Tuniit the first human inhabitants of the Arctic region stretching from Alaska to Greenland, known in the archaeological literature as Palaeo-Eskimos.

Viking the meaning of Norse term *vikingr* remains a subject of debate. The dominant popular understanding is that it originally meant 'pirate', but it may also have denoted raiders or even traders. Pirate raids on England, beginning with Lindisfarne in 793, were deemed to have inaugurated the Viking Age; such raids overlapped with peaceful trading activities. In popular use, public history, and in the heritage and museum sectors, the term is synonymous with 'Norse', despite the fact that the term is gendered (Vikings are always male) and refers to an activity—piracy—that was not characteristic of Norse life in the North Atlantic. In the nineteenth century, and in Anglo-Saxon sources, Vikings were often known as 'Northmen'.

4. Places

Baffin Island (Inuktitut: Qikiqtaaluk) the largest island in the Canadian territory of Nunavut, separated by the Davis Strait from Greenland. It is conventionally identified with the Helluland of the sagas. A possible Norse outpost has been identified on the southern tip of the island at a site known as Tanfield Valley or Nanook.

Brattahlid (Norse: Brattahlíð) in the sagas, the site of Eirik's farm in the Eastern Settlement of Greenland, usually identified with modern Qassiarsuk.

Devon Island (Inuktitut: Tatlurutit) a large island in the Canadian territory of Nunavut, between Baffin Island and Ellesmere Island.

Eastern Settlement (Norse: Eystribyggð) the principal Norse settlement in Greenland, in the fjords at the south-western tip of the island. The name is deceptive, and led early seekers for the remains of the settlement to search on the inhospitable east coast of Greenland.

Eiriksstadir (Norse: Eiríksstaðr; Modern Icelandic: Eiríksstaðir) in the sagas, the farms of Eirik the Red in Haukadalur and Breiðafjörður, in western Iceland.

Ellesmere Island (Inuktitut: Umingmak Nuna) the most northerly island in the Canadian territory of Nunavut, separated from nearby Greenland by Kane Basin and Kennedy Channel. Three Thule sites on the east coast have yielded Norse artefacts.

Gardar (Norse: Garðar; Greenlandic: Igaliku) the seat of the bishop in Greenland. It was established as a residential see in 1124. The last of the nine residential bishops died in 1378, but bishops continued to be appointed until 1537. The see was restored as a titular bishopric in 1996, and the inaugural titular bishop (Edward Clark, a native of Minnesota) was installed in 2001.

Helluland the name (referring etymologically to flat stones) given in the sagas to the land sighted by Bjarni Herjolfsson and later visited by Leif Eirikson and Thorfinn Karlsefni. It is conventionally identified with Baffin Island and adjacent regions of the eastern Canadian Arctic, including Devon Island and Ellesmere Island.

Herjolfsnes (Norse: Herjolfsnæs; Greenlandic Ikigaat), a Norse settlement near the southern tip of Greenland, used as a first port of call by European traders. In the Norse sources it is said to have been settled in the late tenth century by Herjolf Bardarson (Norse: Herjólfr Bárðarson). The late date of some of the clothing excavated in its graveyard may imply that Herjolfsnes was one of the last surviving homesteads in the Eastern Settlement.

Hólar the seat of the episcopal see (from 1106 to 1798) of northern Iceland.

Hop (Norse: Hóp) in the *Saga of Eirik the Red*, the settlement in Vinland established by Thorfinn Karlsefni. The short-lived colony, where Karlsefni's son Snorri was born, was abandoned because of hostile encounters with skrælings.

Hvalsey (Greenlandic: Qaqortukulooq) a farmstead in the Eastern Settlement near modern Qaqortoq. Hvalsey Church is the best preserved Norse ruin in Greenland.

Hvítramannaland (Latin: Albani, English: 'White Man's Land') in the *Saga of Eirik the Red*, a land described by captured skrælings as a country in which people dressed in white. In *Landnámabók*, Hvítramannaland is identified with *Irland it mikla* (Greater Ireland), and said to be located in the west, near Vinland the Good (*þat liggr vestr í haf nær Vínlanndi enu goða*). In the Latin literature, Hvítramannaland is identified with Albani, where the people had white hair and skin.

Leifsbudir (Norse: Leifsbúðir) in the *Saga of the Greenlanders*, the settlement in Vinland established by Leif Eirikson.

Markland the name (referring etymologically to forests) given in the sagas to the land visited by Leif Eirikson and Thorfinn Karlsefni. It is conventionally identified with the coastal area of Labrador (Innu: Nitassinan; Inuit: Nunatsiavut).

Nordseta (Norse: Norðrseta) the northern hunting grounds on the west coast of Greenland, centred on the area around Disko Bay (Greenlandic: Qeqertarsuup tunua).

Ruin Island a small island off the north-west coast of Greenland. The phrase 'Ruin Island Culture' is used to denote the early phase of Thule culture in the eastern high Arctic. Norse artefacts have been found at Thule sites on the island.

Sandnes (Norse: Sandnæs; Greenlandic: Kilaarsarfik) the principal farmstead and the centre of both ecclesiastical and civil authority in the Western Settlement of Greenland.

Skálholt the seat of the episcopal see (from 1056 to 1785) of southern Iceland.

Thingvellir (Norse: Þingvöllr; modern Icelandic: Þingvellir) 'assembly fields', the site in south-west Iceland where the Alþingi met from 930 to 1798.

Snæfellsjökull an extinct volcano on the tip of a peninsula in western Iceland, for centuries used as a navigational marker. In the sagas it is the starting point of Eirik the Red's voyage to Greenland, and is now best known as the entrance to the centre of the earth in Jules Verne's *Voyage au centre de la Terre*.

Thjodhild's Church (Danish: Tjodhildeskirke; Icelandic: Þjóðhildarkirkja) a church excavated at Qassiarsuk, said to have been built by Thjodhild, wife of Eirik the Red.

Vinland in the sagas, the southernmost land discovered and colonized by Leif Eirikson. Philologists assume that the first vowel is long (and so add an acute accent over the 'i') and that the term means 'Land of Wine'. In 1888 a minority view emerged, holding that the first vowel is short, and that the term means 'Land of Meadows'; this view has long been discredited, but survives in popular accounts.

Western Settlement (Norse: Vestribyggð) the Norse settlement on the Nuup Kangerlua fjord on the west coast of Greenland, inland from what is now Nuuk, at the mouth of the fjord. The name is slightly deceptive, in that the settlement is north-north-west of the Eastern Settlement.

5. Sagas and Histories

Descriptio insularum aquilonis (Description of the Northern Islands), the fourth book of *Gesta Hammaburgensis ecclesiae pontificum* (Deeds of the Bishops of Hamburg), a chronicle written in Latin by Adam of Bremen in the late eleventh century. It survives in three versions and many manuscripts, the earliest of which is thirteenth century.

Eiriks saga rauða (*Saga of Eirik the Red*) a saga composed later than *Saga of the Greenlanders*, and perhaps committed to writing in the mid thirteenth century. It survives in two versions: one from the early fourteenth century, and the second (with a superior text) from the late fifteenth century.

Íslendingabók (*Book of Icelanders*) a chronicle, written in Old Norse c. 1200, of the Norse families who settled Iceland in the late ninth and tenth centuries. It was written by Ari Thorgilsson (Ari Þorgilsson), known by his epithet as Ari the Learned (Ari hinn fróði).

Grœnlendinga Saga (*Saga of the Greenlanders*, spelt Grænlendinga Saga in modern Icelandic) a saga probably composed in the twelfth century, and perhaps committed to writing in the thirteenth century. It survives in a late fourteenth-century manuscript.

Landnámabók (*Book of Settlements*) an account by several authors which describes the settlement of Iceland and Greenland by the Norse in the late ninth and tenth centuries. It survives in five medieval versions, the earliest of which (Sturlubók) is late thirteenth century.

6. Languages and Writing Systems

Greenlandic the Inuit language spoken in Greenland. It exists in three dialects: West Greenlandic (Kalaallisut, the official language of Greenland), East Greenlandic (Tunumiisut) and Thule Greenlandic (Inuktun, formerly known as Polar Eskimo). Unlike Canadian varieties of Inuktitut, Greenlandic is written in a Latin script, with additional letters to accommodate loan words from Danish.

Greenlandic Norse an extinct dialect of Old Norse, attested in runic inscriptions in Greenland.

Innu-aimun (French: Montagnais) the Algonquian language spoken by the Innu in Labrador and north-eastern Quebec.

Inuktitut the language (or linguistic continuum) spoken by Inuit people from Alaska to Greenland. The term is sometimes used more narrowly to denote the language of eastern Canada and Greenland, in which case the western Canadian variation is known as Inuvialuktun. The syllabic script of Inuktitut is an adaptation of the Cree script by an Anglican missionary.

Old Norse (also known as Old Icelandic, because most of the sagas were written in Iceland) a North Germanic language spoken in Scandinavia and its overseas colonies from the eighth to the fourteenth centuries. The language was written in runic and Latin alphabets. The descendants of Norse include Norn (the extinct language of Orkney and Shetland) and the modern languages of Danish, Faroese, Icelandic, Norwegian, and Swedish.

Runic a writing system used in parts of northern Europe from late antiquity to modern times. The size and individual characters vary between regions and over time. The earliest letter set, in use until the mid eighth century, had twenty-four characters; the set is known as the Older (or Elder) Futhark (or Fuþark). This early set had an English variant which expanded to thirty characters to accommodate extra vowel sounds; this Anglo-Saxon set is known as the Anglo-Saxon Futhorc. From the mid eighth to the mid eleventh centuries, the period known as the Viking Age, the two principal letter sets (distinguished as 'short-twig' and 'long-branch' forms) each consisted of sixteen characters; they are known as the Younger Futharks. In the Swedish province of Dalarna (known in English as Dalecarlia) another character set was in use from the sixteenth to the early twentieth century.

Tsalagi the Iroquoian language spoken by the Cherokee people. It is written in an eight-five-character syllabary invented in 1821 by a silversmith known in Tsalagi as Sequoyah and in English as George Gist or George Guest. Characters are often derived from the Latin alphabet without reference to their traditional sound values.

FURTHER READING

General

Barnes, Geraldine, *Viking America: The First Millennium* (Cambridge, 2001)

Barraclough, Eleanor Rosamund, *Beyond the Northlands: Viking Voyages and the Old Norse Sagas* (Oxford, 2016)

Bigelow, Gerald (ed), *The Norse of the North Atlantic*, special issue of *Acta Archaeologica* 61 (1990)

Brink, Stefan, and Neil Price (eds), *The Viking World* (London, 2008)

Clunies Ross, Margaret, *The Norse Muse in Britain, 1750–1820* (Trieste, 1998)

Findell, Martin, *Runes* (London, 2014)

Fitzhugh, William W., and Elisabeth I. Ward (eds), *Vikings: The North Atlantic Saga* (Washington and London, 2000)

Lewis-Simpson, Shannon (ed), *Vinland Revisited: The Norse World at the Turn of the First Millennium* (St John's, NL, 2003)

McGhee, Robert, *The Last Imaginary Place: A Human History of the Arctic World* (Oxford, 2004)

Parker, Philip, *The Northmen's Fury: A History of the Viking World* (London, 2014)

Seaver, Kirsten, *The Last Vikings: The Epic Story of the Great Norse Voyagers* (London and New York, 2010)

Wahlgren, Erik, *The Vikings and America* (New York, 1986)

Williams, Gareth, Peter Pentz, and Matthias Wemhoff (eds), *Vikings: Life and Legend* (London, 2014)

Wilson, David, *Vikings and Gods in European Art* (Højbjerg, 1997)

Discovering America

Andersson, Axel, and Scott Magelssen, 'Performing a Viking History of America: The 1893 Voyage and Display of a Viking Longship at the Columbus Quadricentennial.' *Theatre Journal* 69/2 (June 2017), 175–95

Blanck, Dag, 'The Transnational Viking: The Role of the Viking in Sweden, the United States, and Swedish America', in *Journal of Transnational American Studies* 7/1 (2016), 20 pp

Cogley, Richard, 'The Ancestry of the American Indians: Thomas Thorowgood's *Iewes in America* (1650) and *Jews in America* (1660)', *English Literary Renaissance* 35 (2005), 304–30

Feder, Kenneth, *Encylopedia of Dubious Archaeology: From Atlantis to the Walam Olum* (Santa Barbara, CA, 2010)

Feder, Kenneth, *Frauds, Myths, and Mysteries: Science and Pseudoscience in Archaeology* (9th edition, New York, 2018)

Fritze, Ronald H., *Invented Knowledge: False History, Fake Science and Pseudo-Religions* (London, 2009)

Kolodny, Annette, *In Search of First Contact: The Vikings of Vinland, the Peoples of the Dawnland and the Anglo-American Anxiety of Discovery* (Durham, NC, and London, 2012)

Lepper, Bradley, and Jeff Gill, 'The Newark Holy Stones,' *Timeline: A publication of the Ohio Historical Society* 17/3 (2000), 16–25

Mainfort, Robert C., and Mary L. Kwas, "The Bat Creek Stone Revisited: A Fraud Exposed," *American Antiquity* 64 (Oct. 2004), 761–9

Marshall McKusick, *The Davenport Conspiracy Revisited* (Ames, IA, 1991)

Owsley, Douglas W., and Richard L. Jantz (eds), *Kennewick Man: The Scientific Investigation of an Ancient American Skeleton* (College Station, TX, 2014)

Parfitt, Tudor, *The Lost Tribes of Israel: The History of a Myth* (London, 2002)

Rasmussen, Morten, et al., 'The Ancestry and Affiliations of Kennewick Man', *Nature*, 18 June 2015, 455–8

Stanford, Dennis, and Bruce Bradley, *Across Atlantic Ice: The Origins of America's Clovis Culture* (Berkeley and Los Angeles, CA, 2013)

Silverberg, Robert, *The Mound Builders* (Athens, OH, 1986)

Thomas, David, *Skull Wars: Kennewick Man, Archaeology, and the Battle for Native American Identity* (New York, 2001)

Williams, Gwyn, *Madog: The Making of a Myth* (London, 1979)

Sagas and Chronicles

Barnes, Geraldine, 'Vinland the Good: Paradise Lost?', *Paragon* 12/2 (1995), 75–96

Jarus, Owen, 'Archaeologists Closer to Finding Lost Viking Settlement', www.livescience.com, 6 March 2018

Jones, Gwyn, *The Norse Atlantic Saga: Being the Norse Voyages of Discovery and Settlement to Iceland, Greenland, America* (London, 1964; revised edition, 1986)

Sigurðsson, Gísli, *The Medieval Icelandic Saga and Oral Tradition: A Discourse on Method* (Cambridge, MA, 2004)

Maps

Floyd, John Paul, *A Sorry Saga: Theft, Forgery, Scholarship . . . and the Vinland Map* (n.p., 2018)

Larsen, René, and Dorte V. P. Sommer, "Facts and Myths about the Vinland Map and its Context", *Zeitschrift für Kunsttechnologie und Konservierung* 23 (2009), 196–205

Seaver, Kirsten A., *Maps, Myths, and Men: The Story of the Vinland Map* (Stanford, CA, 2004)

Seaver, Kirsten A., "Renewing the Quest for Vinland: The Stefánsson, Resen and Thorláksson Maps", *Mercator's World*, 5/5 (2000), pp. 43–9

Seaver, Kirsten A., 'Saxo Meets Ptolemy: Claudius Clavus and the "Nancy map"', in *Norsk Geografisk Tidsskrift/Norwegian Journal of Geography* 67/2 (2013), pp. 72–86

Skelton, R. A., et al., *The Vinland Map and the Tartar Relation* (2nd edition, New Haven, CT, 1995)

Sommer, Dorte V. P., Axelsson, K. M., et al., "Multiple Microanalyses of a Sample from the Vinland Map", *Archaeometry*, 59 (2017): 287–301

Towe, K. M., R. J. H. Clark, and K. A. Seaver, "Analysing the Vinland Map: A Critical Review of a Critical Review", *Archaeometry* 50 (2008), 887–93

Washburn, Wilcomb E. (ed), *Proceedings of the Vinland Map Conference* (Chicago, 2001)

Iceland and the Discovery of Greenland

Byock, Jesse, *Medieval Iceland: Society, Sagas and Power* (Berkeley, CA, 1988)

Vésteinsson, Orri, *The Christianisation of Iceland: Priests, Power and Social Change 1000–1300* (Oxford, 2000)

Norse Greenland

Arneborg, Jette, Georg Nyegaard, and Orri Vésteinsson, *Norse Greenland: Selected Papers from the Hvalsey Conference, 2008*, special issue of *Journal of the North Atlantic* 2 (2012)

Berglund, Joel, 'Did the Medieval Norse Society in Greenland Really Fail?', in Patricia McAnany and Norman Yoffee, eds, *Questioning Collapse: Human Resilience, Ecological Vulnerability, and the Aftermath of Empire* (Cambridge, 2009), 45–70

Bishop, Rosie R. et al., 'A charcoal-rich horizon at Ø69, Greenland: Evidence for Vegetation Burning during the Norse *landnám*?', *Journal of Archaeological Science* 40 (2013), 3890–902

Dugmore, Andrew, et al., 'Cultural Adaptation, Compounding Vulnerabilities and Conjunctures in Norse Greenland', *PNAS* (Proceedings of the National Academy of Sciences of the United States of America), 109 (2012), 3658–63

Gulløv, Hans Christian, 'The Nature of Contact between Native Greenlanders and Norse', *Journal of the North Atlantic* 1 (2008), 16–24

Hebsgaard, Martin B, et al., '"The Farm Beneath the Sand"–An Archaeological Case Study on Ancient "Dirt" DNA', *Antiquity* 83 (2009), 430–44

Helgason, Agnar, et al., 'Estimating Scandinavian and Gaelic Ancestry in the Male Settlers of Iceland', *American Journal of Human Genetics* 67 (2000), 697–717

Imer, Lisbeth, *Peasants and Prayers: The Inscriptions of Norse Greenland* (Copenhagen, 2017)

Keller, Christian, 'Furs, Fish, and Ivory: Medieval Norsemen at the Arctic Fringe', *Journal of the North Atlantic* 3 (2010), 1–23

Lynnerup, Niels, *The Greenland Norse: A Biological-Anthropological Study* (Copenhagen, 1998)

Molte, I., et al., 'Uncovering the Genetic History of the Present-Day Greenlandic Population', *The American Journal of Human Genetics* 96 (2015), 54–69

Nedkvitne, Arnved, *Norse Greenland: Viking Peasants in the Arctic* (London, 2018)

Ogilvie, Astrid, et al., 'Seals and Sea Ice in Medieval Greenland', *Journal of the North Atlantic* 2 (2009), 60–80

Østergård, Else, *Woven into the Earth: Textiles from Norse Greenland* (2nd edition, Aarhus, 2009)

Palsson, Gisli, 'Genomic Anthropology coming in from the Cold?', *Current Anthropology* 49 (2008), 545–68

Rink, Henry [Hinrich], *Tales and Traditions of the Eskimo* (English translation, Edinburgh and London, 1875)

Roussell, Aage, 'Sandnes and the Neighbouring Farms', *Meddelelser om Grønland* 88/2 (1936), pp. 1–222

Seaver, Kirsten A., *The Frozen Echo: Greenland and the Exploration of North America ca. AD 1000–1500* (Stanford, 1996)

Skaaning-Høegsberg, Mogens, 'A Reassessment of the Development of the Cathedral at Garðar, Greenland', *Archaeologia Islandica* 6 (2007), 74–96

Smith, Michèle Hayeur, Jette Arneborg, and Kevin P. Smith, 'The "Burgundian" Hat from Herjolfsnes, Greenland: New Discoveries, New Dates', *Danish Journal of Archaeology* 4 (2015)

L'Anse aux Meadows

Ingstad, Anne Stine, *The New Land with the Green Meadows* (English translation, St John's, NL 2013)

Ingstad, Helge, *Westward to Vinland: The Discovery of Pre-Columbian Norse House-Sites in North America* (English translation, London, 1969)

Munn, W. A., *Wineland Voyages, Location of Helluland, Markland, and Vinland* (St John's, NL, 1929)

Wallace, Birgitta, 'L'Anse aux Meadows, Leif Eriksson's Home in Vinland', *Journal of the North Atlantic* 2 (2009), 114–25

Wallace, Birgitta, *Westward Vikings: The Saga of L'Anse aux Meadows* (revised edition, St John's, NL, 2012)

The Limits of the Norse Presence in North America

Carpenter, Edmund, *Norse Penny*, (New York, 2003)

Carpenter, Edmund, 'Further Evidence on the Beardmore Relics', *American Anthropologist* 59 (1957), 875–8

Curran, James Watson, *Here Was Vinland; The Great Lakes Region of America* (Sault Ste Marie, ON, 1939)

Currelly, C. T., 'Further Comments Regarding the Beardmore Find', *Canadian Historical Review* 22 (1941), 271–9

Currelly, C. T., 'Viking Weapons Found Near Beardmore, Ontario', *Canadian Historical Review* 20 (1939), 4–7

Elliott, O. C., 'The Case of the Beardmore Relics', *Canadian Historical Review* 22 (1941), 254–71 and 275–709

Gullbekk, Svein, 'The Norse Penny Reconsidered: The Goddard Coin— Hoax or Genuine?', *Journal of the North Atlantic* 33 (2017), 1–8

Harp, Elmer, 'A Late Dorset Copper Amulet from Southeastern Hudson Bay', *Folk: dansk etnografisk tidsskrift: Essays Presented to Helge Larsen on his Seventieth Birthday* 16/17 (1974–75), 33–44

Hunter, Douglas, *Beardmore: The Viking Hoax that Rewrote History* (Montreal and Kingston, 2018)

Laskow, Sarah, 'The Mystery of Maine's Viking Penny', *Atlas Obscura*, 21 December 2017

Liedl, Janice, 'A Canadian Viking in the Governor-General's Court: Medievalism in Pre-War Canada', undated paper on <https://laurentian.academia.edu/JaniceLiedl>

Maxwell, Moreau, *The Prehistory of the Eastern Arctic* (Orlando, FL, 1985)

McKay, Ian, and Robin Bates, *In the Province of History: The Making of the Public Past in Twentieth-Century Nova Scotia* (Montreal and Kingston, 2010)

Montgomery, Ken, 'Banal Race Thinking: Ties of Blood, Canadian History Textbooks and Ethnic Nationalism', *Paedagogica Historica* 41 (2005), 313–36

Mowat, Farley, *The Alban Quest: The Search for a Lost Tribe* (London, 1998), published in North America as *The Farfarers: Before the Norse in North America* (Toronto, 1998)

Mowat, Farley, *Westviking: The Ancient Norse in Greenland and North America* (Boston, 1965)

Park, Robert W., 'Contact between the Norse Vikings and the Dorset Culture in Arctic Canada', *Antiquity* 82 (2008), 189–98

Pringle, Heather, 'Evidence of Viking Outpost Found in Canada', in *National Geographic*, 19 October 2012

Sabo, Deborah, and George Sabo III, 'A Possible Thule Carving of a Viking from Baffin Island, NWT', *Canadian Journal of Archaeology* 2 (1978), 33–42

Schledermann, Peter, 'Notes on Norse Finds from the East Coast of Ellesmere Island, N.W.T.', *Arctic* 33 (1980), 454–63

Sutherland, Patricia, 'The Question of Contact between Dorset Palaeo-Eskimos and Early Europeans in the Eastern Arctic', in H. Maschner, O. Mason, and R. McGhee, eds, *The Northern World AD 900–1400: The Dynamics of Climate, Economy, and Politics in Hemispheric Perspective* (Salt Lake City, 2009), 279–99

Sutherland, Patricia, 'Strands of Culture Contact: Dorset-Norse Interactions in the Canadian Eastern Arctic', in Martin Appelt, et al., eds, *Identities and Cultural Contacts in the Arctic* (Copenhagen, 2000), 159–69

Sutherland, Patricia, Peter Thompson, and Patricia Hunt, 'Evidence of Early Metalworking in Arctic Canada', *Geoarchaeology* 30 (2015), 74–8

Tushingham, A. D., *The Beardmore Relics: Hoax or History* (Toronto, 1966)

American Runestones

Hunter, Douglas, *The Place of Stone: Dighton Rock and the Erasure of America's Indigenous Past* (Chapel Hill, NC, 2017)

Tompsen, Lyle, 'An Archaeologist Looks at the Oklahoma Rune Stones', *Epigraphic Society Occasional Papers* 29 (2011), 5–43

Wahlgren, Erik, 'American Runes: From Kensington to Spirit Pond', *Journal of English and Germanic Philology* 81 (1982), 157–85

Wallace, Birgitta, 'Viking Hoaxes', in Eleanor Guralnick, ed, *Vikings in the West* (Chicago, 1982), pp. 53–76

The Kensington Runestone

Blegen, Theodore, *The Kensington Rune Stone: New Light on an Old Riddle* (St Paul, MN, 1968)

Krueger, David, *Myths of the Runestone: Viking Martyrs and the Birthplace of America* (Minneapolis, MN, 2015)

Merling, Bert, *Alexandria Runestone Pageant, July 4-5-6-7, Winona Lake Amphitheatre, Alexandria, Minnesota* (Alexandria, MN, 1962)

Scholtz, Mike, Lost Conquest <https://youtu.be/i0To9rAfhdI> (2015) [documentary on believers in the Kensington Runestone]

Sprunger, D. A., "Mystery and Obsession: J A Holvik and the Kensington Runestone", *Minnesota History* 57/3 (2000), 140–54

Wahlgren, Erik, *The Kensington Stone, A Mystery Solved* (Madison, WI, 1958)

Williams, Henrik, 'The Kensington Runestone: Fact and Fiction', *The Swedish-American Historical Quarterly* 63/1 (2012), 3–22

Zimmerman, Larry J., 'Unusual or "Extreme" Beliefs about the Past, Community Identity, and Dealing with the Fringe', in Chip Colwell-Chanthaphonh and T. J. Ferguson, eds, *Collaboration in Archaeological Practice: Engaging Descendent Communities* (Plymouth, UK, 2008), 55–86

Understanding Norse America

Clark, David, 'Norse Medievalism in Children's Literature in English', in Margaret Clunies Ross, ed, *The Pre-Christian Religions of the North: Research and Reception, ii: From c. 1830 to the Present* (Turnhout, 2018), 367–400

Haller, William, *Foxe's Book of Martyrs and the Elect Nation* (London, 1963)

Horsman, Reginald, *Race and Manifest Destiny: The Origins of American Racial Anglo-Saxonism* (Cambridge, MA, and London, 1986)

Mancini, J. A., 'Discovering Viking America', *Critical Enquiry* 28 (2002), 868–907

Reid-Merritt, Patricia (ed), *Race in America: How a Pseudoscientific Concept Shaped Human Interaction* (2 vols, Santa Barbara, CA, 2017)

Schultz, April, '"The pride of the race had been touched": The 1925 Norse-American Immigration Centennial and Ethnic Identity', *Journal of American History* 33 (1991), 1265–95

Thomson, Peter, 'Aristotle and King Alfred in America', in Peter Onuf and Nicholas Cole, eds, *Thomas Jefferson, the Classical World, and Early America* (Charlottesville and London, 2011), 193–218

Wawn, Andrew, *The Vikings and the Victorians: Inventing the Old North in Nineteenth-Century Britain* (Woodbridge, 2000)

Woolf, Daniel, *The Idea of History in Early Stuart England* (Toronto, 1990)

PICTURE CREDITS

INDEX

Note: Figures are indicated by an italic "*f*", respectively, following the page number.